BEYOND BOURBON ST.

501
9

Beyond Bourbon St.

An Insider's Guide to New Orleans

2nd Edition

Mark Bologna

Globe Pequot

ESSEX, CONNECTICUT

All information in this guidebook is subject to change. We recommend that you obtain current information before traveling.

Globe Pequot

An imprint of The Globe Pequot Publishing Group, Inc.
64 South Main Street
Essex, CT 06426
www.globepequot.com

Distributed by NATIONAL BOOK NETWORK

British Library Cataloguing in Publication Information available

A previous (2022) edition was catalogued by the Library of Congress as follows:

Names: Bologna, Mark, 1970– author.
Title: Beyond Bourbon St. : an insider's guide to New Orleans / Mark Bologna.
Description: Lanham : Globe Pequot, [2022] | Includes index.
Identifiers: LCCN 2021048603 (print) | LCCN 2021048604 (ebook) |
ISBN 9781493050376 (trade paperback) | ISBN 9781493050383 (epub)
Subjects: LCSH: New Orleans (La.)—Guidebooks.
Classification: LCC F379.N53 B65 2022 (print) | LCC F379.N53 (ebook) |
DDC 917.63/3504—dc23/eng/20211007
LC record available at https://lccn.loc.gov/2021048603
LC ebook record available at https://lccn.loc.gov/2021048604

ISBN 978-1-4930-8985-7 (paper : alk. paper)
ISBN 978-1-4930-8986-4 (electronic)

Printed in India

For Marie, Olivia, and Sophia

St. Louis Cathedral JAMES CULLEN

Café Du
Monde

CONTENTS

Krewe of Bacchus JAMES CULLEN

Jackson Square/St. Louis Cathedral JAMES CULLEN

INTRODUCTION

New Orleans is so much more than the Bourbon Street scenes you see on the national news once a year on Mardi Gras. It's a 300-year-old city made up of vibrant neighborhoods, diverse populations, and traditions layered upon each other.

World-class food is available not only in our famous restaurants, but also in corner restaurants throughout the city. Mardi Gras is the party we throw for ourselves, but invite the world to take part in. If partying with millions of friends is not your style, there are festivals nearly every week of the year to suit your taste and interests.

The challenge? There is much more to New Orleans than meets the eye.

If you're not careful, you'll spend too much of your time on Bourbon Street, or in the nearby run-of-the-mill tourist shops. Sure, you'll have a good time, but you'll miss the essence of New Orleans. It's not hard to have a completely different experience, if you know where to go and what to eat, see, and do. What you need is a local, a New Orleanian, who can point you in the right direction, explain how to pronounce our street names, and save you time.

It's easy to come to the Crescent City and never venture far from Bourbon Street. That's a mistake. While our famous street deserves your attention, there is far more to explore, and none of it is far away.

For instance, you can hear good music on Bourbon Street, or you can walk over to Preservation Hall and hear the best traditional jazz musicians in the world playing together with the newer generation. Or you can walk over to Buffa's Bar at the downtown edge of the French Quarter and enjoy a cheap meal, a good drink, and music that will soothe your soul. Your choice.

In this book, we'll help you explore New Orleans based on the advice of insiders, locals like me. You'll learn how to make the most of your time, how best to experience the city, and what to do when you're torn between this or that. We'll point out the things we'd show you if you came to visit us for a weekend, a week, or a month! We've done this for more than 30 years for our friends, and for the last several years through the *Beyond Bourbon Street* podcast. Sit back, relax, and get ready to have the time of your life.

Laissez les bons temps rouler!

—Mark Bologna

PLANNING YOUR TRIP AND GETTING AROUND

When someone decides to visit a place like New Orleans, there is something special about being able to refer to a book—to mark it up, to immerse yourself in it, and to make the destination your own.

I have lived most of my life in this city and can tell visitors what is most important at Mardi Gras (answer: a place to pee) and where to find it (answer: churches along the parade route are often open and allow visitors free access to restrooms; schools also open up and offer a clean restroom in exchange for a nominal fee).

I can explain how to avoid the crowds at Jazz Fest, where to get out of the sun, and which stages are the best for their interests. I

Bologna family at Mardi Gras **MARK BOLOGNA**

could go on, but the point is I have a depth of knowledge not often found in those other guides.

I do not intend this guide to be a complete list of everything. Instead, it will be curated to save you from being overwhelmed.

I want this guide to be a reference, as if you were getting information from your friend who is a local. I want the writing to be simple, fun, and engaging. I want most people to be able to read the text without reading glasses, and to easily find what they need when they need it.

My original intent was to write this book with sections titles, "Eat," "See," "Do." As I went about writing, I realized New Orleans is about neighborhoods. I decided to shift and tell the story of New Orleans through its neighborhoods, and within those help you find the places to eat, the things to do, and what you should see. Most of all I came to realize that my goal is to help you experience New Orleans.

We'll explore New Orleans in the way I would take you around.

WHEN SHOULD I VISIT?

Deciding when to visit New Orleans is often a reflection of where you live. Sure, vacation schedules, the school year, and other factors play a role, but the weather you are accustomed to and prefer should influence when to come.

WEATHER

New Orleans doesn't have much of a winter or fall. We basically have summer and some combination of fall and spring without the changing colors found in many other places. When it is cooler the dampness can make it feel much colder than the thermometer might indicate. Locals refer to it as a damp cold.

Beginning in May the weather is typically hot and humid. This combination reaches its peak in August or September, but early October is often still warm. November through February are the coldest months, though it is not unusual for the temperatures to jump into the upper 70s or even to reach 80. It feels like we have two to four weeks of spring at best before the heat and humidity return.

Hurricane season runs from June through November. I would not let this scare you away, but just be aware when planning your visit. The major issue with hurricanes in New Orleans tends to be street flooding. Since half of the city sits below sea level, our streets can only drain when the pumps are working and can pull the water down the drains and out into the canals that snake through the city. If the rain falls too quickly or in too much volume, the pumps cannot keep up and the streets will flood until they do.

AVERAGE WEATHER BY MONTH

MONTH	HIGH/LOW TEMPERATURE	RAIN
Jan	64°F/45°F	7 days
Feb	66°F/47°F	6 days
Mar	73°F/54°F	5 days
Apr	79°F/61°F	4 days
May	85°F/68°F	4 days
June	90°F/74°F	10 days
July	92°F/76°F	11 days
Aug	92°F/76°F	12 days
Sept	88°F/72°F	8 days
Oct	81°F/65°F	5 days
Nov	72°F/53°F	5 days
Dec	65°F/46°F	6 days

When it does rain, you can usually expect afternoon showers that sometimes turn into thunderstorms. Often the rain is limited to a light shower and won't impact your exploration too much.

NEW ORLEANS SEASONS: CRAWFISH, FESTIVALS, SUMMER, AND SAINTS

New Orleanians like to say our seasons are Crawfish, Festivals, Summer, and Saints. Crawfish season begins right around Christmas but doesn't really kick into gear until March or so depending on how the weather has been in the late months of the previous year. Temperature and rainfall have a big impact on the crop.

Boiled crawfish **MARK BOLOGNA**

Festival season kicks off with the French Quarter Festival in April followed by Jazz Fest. As we head into summer, there is a steady stream of events both small and large. The calendar is

Mardi Gras at night JAMES CULLEN

full through October. Summer is hot and humid but brings with it smaller crowds and plenty of sun. If you can stand the heat, it can be a nice time to visit, especially if you can match your trip to one of the smaller festivals.

Rooms rates are cheaper in the summer months, with August being a traditionally slow time of year.

By the time September rolls around, talk turns to the Saints. New Orleans loves the Saints, and you'll notice the difference when they win or lose on Mondays after game days.

ARRIVAL AND DEPARTURE

AIRPORT

Louis Armstrong New Orleans International Airport (MSY) is the main airport in New Orleans. Lakefront is mostly used by private planes. The next nearest airport is in Gulfport, Mississippi, which may be an option if you plan to rent a car and visit the Gulf Coast.

In November 2019, MSY opened a new set of terminals that completely replaced the old structure. The "new airport" features modern amenities, including local restaurants and shops. The rental car counters and long-term parking are a bit farther away than before. If this is your first trip to New Orleans since November 2019, allow more time than you did in the past. On the positive side, the process of going through security is quicker than before. CLEAR and TSA PreCheck are both available at the terminal.

GETTING FROM THE AIRPORT

In most cases, you'll be staying in or near the French Quarter. The ride from MSY is 15 to 30 minutes depending on traffic. Your options include taxi, rideshare, shuttle, or rental car. In our experience, a rideshare will be the quickest and most pleasant. If you are on a budget or staying at one of the large hotels, a shuttle may be the way to go.

Uber and **Lyft** operate in New Orleans. After you exit the plane, look for the baggage claim signs. You'll go down to the first floor, then look for the rideshare signs. The door you need should be on your left.

PRE-TRIP CHECKLIST

Before you leave home, there are some things you want to keep in mind to make your trip a success.

First on my list is reservations. If you plan on taking a tour, dining at one of our more popular restaurants, attending a special event, or booking a balcony on Bourbon Street for a night of revelry, make sure you take care of those reservations ahead of time. The same goes for anything you truly have your heart set on doing.

With more than 1,400 restaurants in New Orleans, there are always alternative options and often the concierge at your hotel will be able to make last-minute reservations for you, but why chance it? The same goes for event tickets like Saints and Pelicans games, concerts, etc. You might get lucky and score tickets on the resale market, but popular events are often sold out.

WHAT SHOULD I PACK?

Some things are universal for any trip, but the following items are essential for a visit to New Orleans. (*Note:* Mardi Gras comes with its own special list of things you'll need. If you are visiting during that time of year, you'll find a checklist in the Mardi Gras chapter.)

Comfortable walking shoes. New Orleans is best explored on foot, so comfortable shoes are a must. The French Quarter is often less than spotless, so it is also a good idea to have a closed shoe option that you don't mind getting dirty. For Jazz Fest you can get away with flip-flops, but these are not a good idea for general sightseeing.

A brimmed hat. The sun can be scorching even if the temperatures are mild. Nothing can ruin your visit faster than a sunburn.

Sunscreen. See above. Sunscreen is especially needed when attending outdoor festivals like the French Quarter Festival and Jazz Fest. The latter offers little shade, which means hours basking/baking in the sun. Be prepared.

A rain jacket and/or umbrella. Rain showers tend to pop up suddenly. Lots of New Orleans is best enjoyed outdoors. These items will ensure you can still explore even on wet days.

SHOULD I RENT A CAR?

In most cases, there will be no need for you to rent a car. New Orleans is best experienced on foot or by riding on the streetcar. If you do not want to walk or have physical challenges, a rideshare or taxi can get you where you need to go for $5 to $15 in most cases.

Hotel parking is expensive. Meters have two-hour limits and are active until 8 p.m. in some places. During peak tourist seasons and special events, you'll have more hassles than you need for a vehicle that will likely only be used to get to and from the airport, and perhaps to dinner. Save the dollars and your time. Exceptions to this point are if you plan to visit the Gulf Coast or a plantation. Even then, I would rent a car for only the days you need it. Rental cars are available at several downtown locations and through some hotels.

GEOGRAPHY MATTERS: GETTING AROUND NEW ORLEANS

Let's head in a different direction and talk about geography. I didn't know it when I started the *Beyond Bourbon Street* podcast, but giving directions on how to get somewhere in New Orleans has been one of my greatest challenges.

The problem is that New Orleanians don't use compass directions. Instead, everything is downtown, uptown, by the lake, or by the river. To make it even more confusing, downtown to a New Orleanian really means downriver, so downtown can mean "past" what you would think of as downtown, or in our case the Central Business District. You still with me? In case that isn't confusing enough, you might've noticed the river curves, so towards the river does not imply north, west, east, or south.

Ask a New Orleanian for directions and you'll often get this: Go down Magazine Street towards Uptown. The place you want is on the lake side of the street, in the Lower Garden District, just past the Jackson Avenue.

I just described how to get to Stein's Deli from the Central Business District. If you had asked me if that was west or south, I would have given you a blank stare and a shrug.

Some New Orleanians add "backatown" as a direction. To get your head around this, think of the French Quarter, the original footprint of the city. The streets closest to the river are the front of town. The French Quarter ends at Rampart Street in one direction. This is headed towards Lake Pontchartrain. Back of Rampart Street is the Tremé—one of the oldest neighborhoods outside the French Quarter. This was considered backatown. Trombone Shorty even named one of his albums *Backatown* since that is where he grew up: in the Tremé, behind the city, the French Quarter.

MANAGING EXPECTATIONS

Match your plan and your expectations with the interests of your group and you'll have a great time!

If someone is interested in history, the WWII Museum would be a great choice. Foodies will have their pick of hole-in-the-wall eateries to fine dining. Outdoor enthusiasts might enjoy City Park.

I believe this is the key for all adventures, whether you are by yourself, with that special someone, or with the entire family. Spend a little time discussing or thinking about each member of your party, then try to match what you do with their preferences.

I think this is especially true in New Orleans: this is a place where people, young and old, can get easily overwhelmed—with the crowds, the sights, the sounds. True sensory overload.

Take, for example, my own daughters. Olivia loves to be in the thick of things: when we go to festivals, we have to watch because she'll dart between people to get right up close to the performers. One year, she begged to go on stage while the Mardi Gras Indians were performing. Sophia, however, once asked me if I could take Olivia to Jazz Fest, but not her, because of the crowds. She simply doesn't like them—well, except at Mardi Gras, then she's fine. In any event, my advice is to try to find the things that best match each person. Hopefully, you'll find enough overlap!

St. Louis Cathedral and Jackson Square **JAMES CULLEN**

Cityscape along the Mississippi River **JAMES CULLEN**

Of course, as the city expanded, backatown did, too. It eventually also absorbed Midcity and Gentilly. It gets confusing because at some point the intersection of Uptown and Downtown runs into backatown. For our purposes, backatown commonly means the Tremé and can include Midcity.

All of this gets me back to my point about giving you directions. I try to translate in my head, as best I can, the directions I've grown up with into north, south, east, and west for you. Post-Katrina we have more transplants, so I hear some people using compass directions, but it is an immediate giveaway you didn't grow up here. The reverse is also true: when I moved from New Orleans to Minnesota years ago, I had no idea what direction north was when people would tell me to head north to get here or there. I have the same problem with my car's GPS.

Imagine sitting on a park bench on the Moonwalk, the promenade next to the Mississippi River across from Jackson Square. You're gazing at the river traffic, and you notice a point of land out there, just a bit to the left. That's Algiers Point. Pronounced al-JEERS. It's over there on the West Bank. What? The west bank of the river. The French Quarter is on the East Bank. Pull out your phone and see what compass direction that is. It's east!

In New Orleans, everything south of Lake Pontchartrain is considered to be on the east bank of the river, while the other side of the river is considered to be the west bank.

My family would tell you no matter what that I have no sense of direction, whether I am using a compass, New Orleans directions, or even my phone's GPS. They're right. As a result of all this, giving you directions is the hardest part of the podcast and was a challenge in writing this book, but I did it anyway. You're welcome. I love you.

Nighttime view **JAMES CULLEN**

MAPS

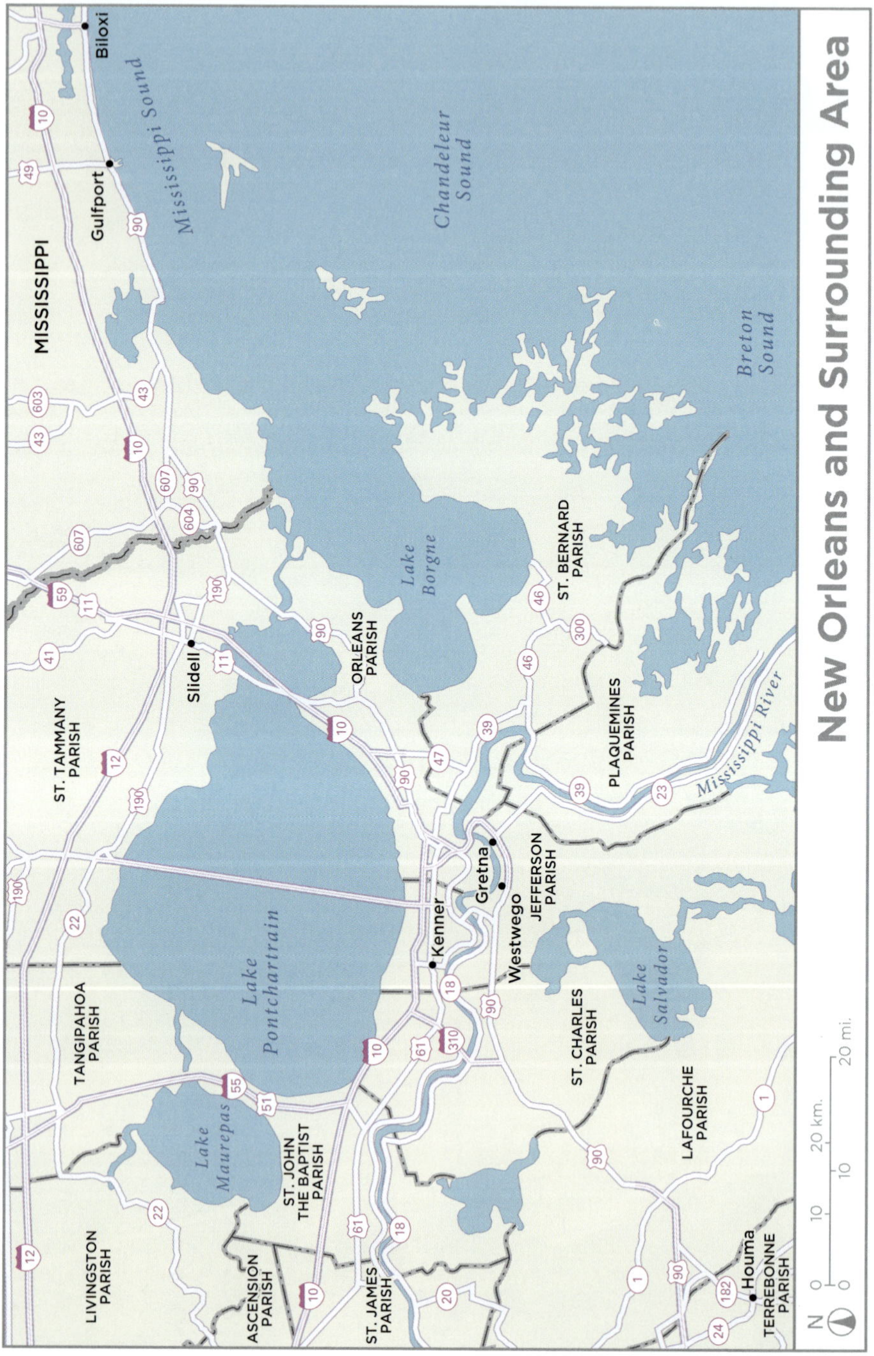
New Orleans and Surrounding Area
MISSISSIPPI
Biloxi
Gulfport
Mississippi Sound
Chandeleur Sound
Breton Sound
Lake Borgne
Lake Pontchartrain
Lake Maurepas
Lake Salvador
Mississippi River
Slidell
Kenner
Gretna
Westwego
Houma
ST. TAMMANY PARISH
ORLEANS PARISH
ST. BERNARD PARISH
PLAQUEMINES PARISH
JEFFERSON PARISH
ST. CHARLES PARISH
LAFOURCHE PARISH
TERREBONNE PARISH
TANGIPAHOA PARISH
LIVINGSTON PARISH
ASCENSION PARISH
ST. JOHN THE BAPTIST PARISH
ST. JAMES PARISH
0 10 20 km.
0 10 20 mi.
N

Metropolitan New Orleans

Close-up of Metropolitan New Orleans

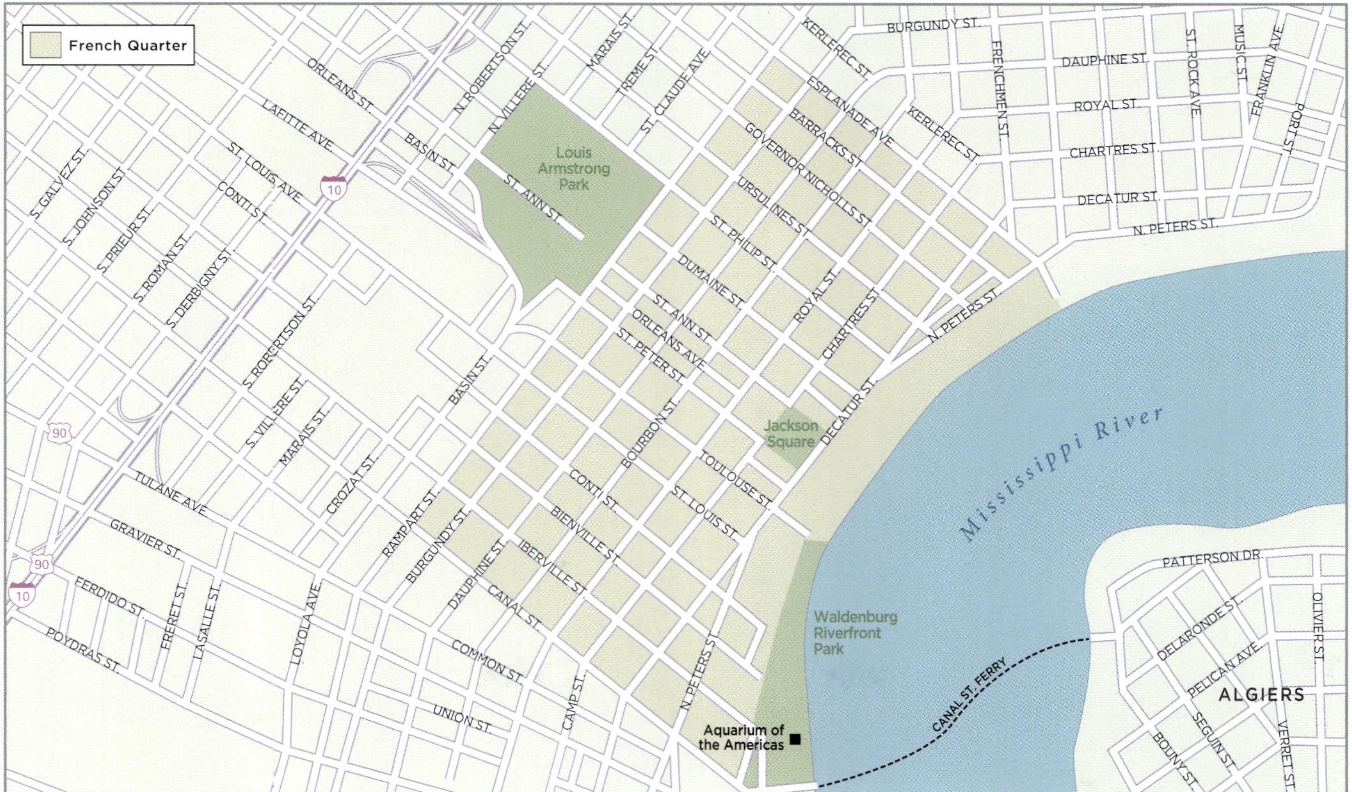

French Quarter

Purple fleur-de-lis PIERRE LONGNUS/GETTY IMAGES

LET'S TALK LANGUAGE, Y'ALL

If you've been to New Orleans, you might've noticed we talk differently. This chapter will help you get a flavor of the city, learn a little about the history, and know what you're getting into when you come to visit!

New Orleans owes its colorful language to the mix of cultures that make the city what it is: French, Spanish, African, Creole, Cajun, and the people of Nova Scotia, Haiti, and the Caribbean as a whole. We're influenced by our colonial roots, the slave trade, our food, and our music.

As I put this chapter together, I realized the uniqueness of the language of New Orleans crosses many different topics, including places, food, terms of endearment, everyday items, Mardi Gras, and even colors.

We'll cover some of the terms that hit the intersection of commonly used in New Orleans *and* unique and interesting. You'll hear these things frequently in New Orleans and maybe not have heard them in other places. Or you might've heard them but weren't quite sure what they meant or why they were used.

There are enough unique words and colloquialisms for more than one chapter. In fact, this topic could probably be a small book. This chapter will at least cover the items you are most likely to hear from locals during your visit.

Enough of a preface. Let's jump into the language of New Orleans.

The word **lagniappe** (lan-YAPP) is a good starting point on our journey through the verbal landscape of New Orleans. It's one of my favorite words, not only because of what it means but because of its origin and specifically that it brings together so many New Orleans influences, all in one word.

In New Orleans lagniappe means "a little something extra." Mark Twain refers to lagniappe as "a word worth traveling to New Orleans to get" in his book *Life on the Mississippi*.

The word entered English from the Louisiana French, who adapted a Quechua (catch-wah) word brought to New Orleans by the Spanish Creoles. It derived from the South American Spanish term *la yapa* or *ñapa* (referring to a free extra item, usually a very cheap one). And, just to tie it into New Orleans's Catholic heritage, Quechua was the language used by the Roman Catholic missionaries in Central America after the Spanish conquest in the 16th century.

The term has been traced back to the Quechua word *yapay* ("to increase; to add"). In Andean markets it is still customary to ask for a *yapa* (translates as "a little extra") when making a purchase. The seller usually responds by throwing in a little extra.

In this guide, lagniappe means an extra tip, historical note, or additional piece of information: something you weren't expecting but hopefully will appreciate and enjoy. At dinner, it is the New Orleans equivalent of an amuse-bouche, though it might be offered at the end of the meal.

As a kid I would frequently go to the French Market with my mom or dad to purchase cases of fresh vegetables for our restaurant. The vendors would almost always offer an extra piece of fruit for me to eat or sometimes another few tomatoes, a few heads of lettuce . . . lagniappe.

New Orleans used to have a daily newspaper named the *Times Picayune*. On Fridays, the *Picayune* would have a pullout section called Lagniappe, which was a guide to the events of the upcoming weekend.

Now, let's talk about **New Orleans** itself.

New Orleans is pronounced New Or-LUNS or New Or-LEE-UNS by locals. Almost never New or-LEANS and definitely not N'AW-LINS. One exception: the late Frank Davis, a local TV personality, sportsman, cook, and all-around great guy, used to have a segment on the local news called "Naturally N'Awlins." Frank could get away with it. You (and I) shouldn't.

We have several nicknames for the city. **Big Easy** refers to the laid-back vibe of the city. **Crescent City** is a nod to the bend in the river against which the city of New Orleans was established in 1718.

New Orleans is also referred to as the **City That Care Forgot.** The meaning appears to be lost to history, but the term was first used in the 1930s. And, of course, New Orleans is often referred to as **NOLA,** short for New Orleans, Louisiana.

Another essential and unique New Orleans term is **neutral ground:** it's the median in most parts of the United States, but not here in New Orleans.

Any discussion of the neutral ground must first start with Canal Street. Its name refers to plans for a canal that would connect the Mississippi River with Lake Pontchartrain. The plans were abandoned and the canal was never dug.

Today, Canal Street is a major thoroughfare in the city and is one boundary of the French Quarter. It has three lanes in each direction and a wide space in the middle where the streetcar tracks and buses run today.

Canal Street separates the French Quarter from the Central Business District, or the area of the city known as the American Sector in the early 1800s. Back then the French Quarter was populated by the Creoles, while Americans, largely from the Midwest, moved to the city and lived Uptown.

Since the street and the canal were going to be in between the two distinct populations, the middle became known as the neutral ground, almost certainly a nod to the cultural divide. While the canal never came to be, the phrase stuck, and eventually neutral ground became the accepted term for any median in New Orleans.

Here's a little lagniappe! During Mardi Gras you will hear sides of the parade referred to as either the sidewalk side or the neutral ground side. As in, "I am riding in Endymion, 16th float, neutral ground side." Or, "I'll see you at the parades tonight, on the corner of Napoleon and St. Charles, neutral ground side." You can even get T-shirts that say "sidewalk side" or "neutral ground side."

Next up, let's talk about counties that aren't. In Louisiana we don't have counties, we have **parishes.** Ever wonder why?

Louisiana was officially Roman Catholic under both Spanish and French rule. Boundaries separating territories generally matched church parishes. In 1807 the Louisiana legislature formally adopted the term "parish" and it's been that way ever since.

In 1816 the first official map of the state used the term "parish," as did the 1845 constitution. Since then the official term for Louisiana's primary civil divisions has been "parish." We have 64 of them today including Orleans, which encompasses New Orleans and was named after the Duke of Orléans, the Regent of France.

We have one parish, Chalmette, that is also lovingly referred to as **da' parish.** People who grew up in Chalmette, just downriver from the French Quarter by a couple of miles, have a unique dialect and are known locally as **Yats.** As in, "Where y'at, dawlin'?" They are honored and imitated in song, in speech, and even in cartoon.

My favorite parish name is Evangeline, named for the Acadian heroine of Henry Longfellow Wadsworth's poem "Evangeline." I tried to get my wife to name one of our girls Evangeline, but I was unsuccessful.

Next up are **shotgun houses.** These are part of the architectural identity of New Orleans. The term refers to a narrow rectangular house, with rooms one behind the other and doors at either end of the structure. They are usually no more than 12 feet wide. The name "shotgun" refers to the idea of being able to fire a shotgun blast from the front door and have the shot travel all the way through the building without hitting a wall.

The shotgun was the most popular style of house in the southern United States from the end of the Civil War until the 1920s. One variation, at least in New Orleans, is the **camelback,** which has a second-story addition near the back half of the house.

The origins of shotgun houses are somewhat murky: some suggest they originated in the Creole faubourgs (neighborhoods) of New Orleans in the early 1800s. Others suggest the shotgun house has its origins in Haiti. In any event, there were definitely shotgun houses present in New Orleans by the 1830s, if not earlier.

Example of a shotgun house **MARK BOLOGNA**

Usually the front room is a living room or parlor, followed by one or two bedrooms. The kitchen is typically the last room in the house. Since the style predates indoor plumbing, bathrooms were added on later, usually as an offset to the kitchen or sometimes just in front of the kitchen. Today, if you look for it, you can often see the addition attached to the kitchen.

Shotgun houses have small front porches and are close to the street, with little or no front yard. This setup allows good airflow, which is another reason the doorways going from room to room are all lined up. Additionally, shotgun houses in New Orleans are raised slightly, usually 3 or 4 feet off the ground. This feature also helps with air circulation.

Another variation is the **double shotgun,** which is essentially two houses under one roof that share a center wall. You'll also see double shotguns that have been renovated and are now the residence of a single family.

You can find examples of shotgun houses throughout New Orleans, ranging from the very small and simple to fairly elaborate and quite large, especially if doubles have been converted into one residence and have a camelback.

Faubourg is a word I used a few paragraphs earlier. It is an old French word that loosely means "suburb." In New Orleans the term is used to describe the neighborhoods beyond the French Quarter, so not really suburbs in the sense you would think of them today. There are 73 areas in the city recognized as neighborhoods, or faubourgs, though many of them have names locals do not recognize as "official."

Two of the oldest New Orleans neighborhoods outside the French Quarter are the Faubourg Marigny and the Faubourg Tremé. The Marigny is one of the oldest parts of the city outside the French Quarter. It is just downriver of the French Quarter and was founded in 1805.

The Marigny is a popular destination within the city for both entertainment and as a place to live. It includes Frenchmen Street, which is lined with live music venues and restaurants. The Marigny also has a unique and colorful architectural style, combining elements of our French, Spanish, and Caribbean, predominantly Haitian, heritage. You will find cottages and shotgun houses in bright colors with lots of architectural details.

The Tremé is one of the oldest neighborhoods in New Orleans and is considered the oldest African-American neighborhood in the United States. It is located just behind the French Quarter, once you cross Rampart Street.

You can often see second line parades and jazz funerals in the Tremé. It also includes Armstrong Park, a tribute to the great Louis Armstrong. Within the park is Congo Square.

Congo Square was considered the town center of the Tremé, and was a gathering place for slaves in the 18th and 19th centuries. It was a place they could go on Sundays to dance, play music, and trade. Congo Square was also the original home of the New Orleans Jazz Festival in 1970.

Within the confines of Armstrong Park is the Mahalia Jackson Performing Arts Theater, home of the New Orleans Philharmonic and the Opera Association and host to numerous Broadway shows and traveling music acts throughout the year.

Let's shift from places to a discussion of the terms **Cajun** and **Creole.** These are both used to refer to people and to styles of food. Cajun refers to the French Acadians who were exiled from Nova Scotia by the British for their Catholic beliefs during the French and Indian

War. Many settled in Louisiana, and more specifically along the bayous southwest of New Orleans. This area encompasses 22 parishes today, in an area referred to as Acadiana.

The Cajuns were relatively isolated in their new home, but this worked out OK because they were able to use the trapping, hunting, fishing, and pig farming skills they brought with them. Those influences are definitely noticeable in Cajun food today: it tends to be hearty and a bit rustic. That's not to say it isn't good—it's great, in fact, just not typically fancy.

Creole, however, is more complicated. The word is derived from the Spanish *criollo* (cre-ol-YO), which means "native to a place." The term "Creole" usually refers to city people, and traditionally in New Orleans, those of French, Spanish, African, or Caribbean ancestry. It is also sometimes used in New Orleans to refer to those of mixed race and/or to those of African descent who were born here as opposed to those who came here as slaves.

In terms of food, Creole tends to mean French in heritage, but it typically includes influences from several cultures, all part of our heritage. From Spanish cooking, the bell peppers, onions, and celery known as the **holy trinity.** A close cousin is the French **mirepoix**: onions, carrots, and celery.

Sicilian immigrants contributed tomatoes, which are integral to so many sauces in New Orleans cuisine. Filé comes from the Native Americans, and okra is African: both are used as thickeners in our beloved gumbo. Cayenne pepper, ubiquitous to so many New Orleans dishes, is Caribbean. Again, native to a place or a people. You blend this together and you get native to New Orleans. If Creole seems a little fuzzier than Cajun, that's because it is.

The differences in the food might seem subtle if you're not from New Orleans. For instance, many Cajun and Creole dishes start with a **roux:** a blend of fat, usually oil or butter, and flour. However, Cajun roux tends to be darker and more intense. It takes longer to prepare. When I make a dark roux for a gumbo, it can take 45 minutes of constant stirring to get just the right color and depth.

In contrast, Creole roux tends to be lighter, though there are exceptions to everything. A Creole roux is sometimes almost blond, like what you would make as a base for étouffée.

You can see and taste the difference in jambalaya, too. Cajun jambalaya is typically brown; the color comes from the bits that are scraped up from the bottom of the cast-iron pot while you are cooking. Jambalaya made in the Creole tradition is typically red, thanks to the introduction of the tomato.

For the most part Cajun food was not common in New Orleans until **Paul Prudhomme** brought it to the city in the 1970s. Today, many chefs carry on the tradition, including Donald Link at Cochon, his restaurant in the Warehouse District.

Two of my favorite cookbooks help illustrate the differences between Cajun and Creole. Chef Paul Prudhomme's *Louisiana Kitchen* cookbook is the epitome of a Cajun cookbook. In contrast, Richard and Rima Collin's *New Orleans Cookbook* contains many dishes with the same names as those found in Prudhomme's, but the preparation and the ingredients sometimes vary significantly.

If you can find these two cookbooks, they are a terrific start to any collection about New Orleans and Louisiana cooking in general. Both of mine have numerous stains and marks in them from years of use.

I have the best of both worlds. I was born and raised in New Orleans. My last name is Bologna: my dad's family is Sicilian, while my mom's is French and German. I went to college deep in Acadiana, in Lafayette. While only 140 miles from my present home in the heart of New Orleans, I definitely experienced the difference between Creole and Cajun. Everything from the food to the music to the dialects and cultures. If you get the chance, you should spend some time in Cajun country.

Let's stick with food for a minute. I mentioned roux, but let's run through several other terms you'll come across in New Orleans.

Here, **dressed** isn't a reference to your clothing but instead refers to how you want your po-boy. Dressed typically means lettuce, tomatoes, mayo, and pickles. If you are ordering a seafood po-boy, then it also means ketchup and hot sauce. If you ask for mustard, you usually need to specify yellow or Creole, sometimes called hot mustard.

You come across ***cochon de lait*** at Jazz Fest, school fairs, and certainly in Cajun country. It roughly translates to "suckling pig." A *cochon de lait* also generally refers to the roasting of a pig. At Jazz Fest, one of the more popular dishes is a *cochon de lait* po-boy: shredded, roasted pork on po-boy bread. Delicious!

Ya-ka-mein is a noodle soup, made typically with the addition of beef, green onions, and a boiled egg. Known as "Old Sober," it is frequently sold outside late-night clubs to

Cochon de lait po-boy **MARK BOLOGNA**

patrons who may have imbibed too much. You'll also find it at some neighborhood corner stores and sold out of the back of pickup trucks during second lines. The most famous version of this fusion of Asian and African-American cuisine is made by Miss Linda Green.

Gumbo Ya Ya is one of my favorite New Orleans dishes. It refers to chicken and andouille gumbo. My favorite version can be found at Mr. B's Bistro in the French Quarter. It has a dark, rich roux and strong andouille.

Speaking of **andouille,** this is a smoked pork sausage made with pork butt, fat, salt, black pepper, and garlic. It is traditionally smoked over pecan wood. LaPlace, Louisiana, just west of New Orleans, is nicknamed the Andouille Capital of the World. You'll find andouille sausage used in many New Orleans dishes, including gumbo and jambalaya.

Before we move on, any conversation that mentions Mr. B's Bistro must include BBQ shrimp.

BBQ shrimp JAMES CULLEN

BBQ shrimp is a dish that originated at Pascale's Manale in Uptown New Orleans. Despite the name, it does not include BBQ sauce. Instead, it consists of shrimp sautéed in a sauce of butter, lemon, Worcestershire sauce, garlic, cracked black pepper, and Creole seasoning. It is typically served with plenty of hot French bread for dipping.

The shrimp are usually served unpeeled and with the heads on. This makes BBQ shrimp messy to eat. Some restaurants will remove the shells if you ask, and they'll furnish a bib or an extra cloth napkin if you need it.

BBQ shrimp is one of my favorite dishes, and I am partial to the ones they serve at Mr. B's Bistro. In fact, it's on my last-meal menu. You know, the menu I would eat if I knew I had only one dinner left? In New Orleans we live to eat, not eat to live. This is yet another "only in New Orleans" saying now that I think about it.

Next up, **crawfish.** Not crayfish, not crawdad, and never mudbugs. Act like a local and call them crawfish. If you get the chance to eat boiled crawfish, remember to not eat the ones whose tails are sticking straight out. It means they were dead before they hit the water, which is not a good thing.

Boiled crawfish **JAMES CULLEN**

Besides boiled, you'll find crawfish in gumbo, étouffée, and bisque. Sometimes, you'll find a fried crawfish tail po-boy. My favorite is a combination of crawfish étouffée with fried crawfish on top. It's the way I make it at home. Something about the crispiness of the fried crawfish on top of the étouffée makes it extra special.

That leads us to **étouffée,** pronounced EH-too-FAY. Étouffée refers to a method of cooking meat or seafood by smothering it with vegetables, usually celery, bell peppers, and onions. In New Orleans the typical étouffée is shrimp or crawfish, and is served over rice. Similar to gumbo, étouffée is made with a roux, but it is a blond or light roux as I described earlier.

In contrast, most gumbos are made with a medium to dark roux. The difference is achieved by the cooking time of the roux. The darker the roux, the more intense the flavor of the dish. Shrimp étouffée typically includes a tomato-based sauce, while crawfish étouffée does not.

Let's talk about **pecans.** They are not pee-cans, at least not in New Orleans. Pee-cans are those portable potties you use at Jazz Fest and Mardi Gras. Nothing will expose you as a visitor quicker than to ask for pee-can pie.

I can't think about pecans without thinking about **pralines.** The praline was originally a French confection made with sugar and almonds. After their arrival in New Orleans in the mid-1700s, local candymakers quickly substituted native pecans for the almonds. Combined with our plentiful local sugarcane, it was a natural fit. While other places have them, New Orleans pralines are made most often with pecans, sugar, and cream.

You undoubtedly know about **beignets,** the popular French-style fried doughnuts made famous by Cafe du Monde. But what about café au lait? **Café au lait** is coffee and chicory mixed with scalded milk. Chicory is actually a weed with a bitter taste. It was and is used as an extender in coffee. Rather than being seen as a negative, coffee and chicory is very popular in New Orleans. When combined with beignets at Cafe du Monde or Cafe Beignet, it makes a perfect pair. The bitterness of the chicory helps offset the sweetness of the powdered sugar on the beignets.

Hubig's pies are fried pies filled with fruit. Lemon is the best, but they also come in apple, coconut, chocolate, pineapple, sweet potato, and sometimes other varieties. We had these in place of a groom's cake when my wife and I were married in 2009. Instead of the normal label at the top, they were adorned with *Mark & Marie* and the date.

The bakery burned down in 2012, but it returned to business in November 2022. As I mentioned, lemon is the best, though my wife believes it is apple. She's wrong, but I love her anyway.

Now, let's discuss **go cups.** A go cup refers to a plastic cup given to patrons as they leave a bar in New Orleans. New Orleans allows open containers: that is, you can walk around town with an open container and drink alcohol, as long as it isn't in a glass bottle. If you want to leave a bar and finish your drink on the street, just ask for a go cup.

"Go cup" is also the term locals use to describe the plastic cups you catch as throws during Mardi Gras. Those cups tend to be made of a sturdier plastic than what you get leaving a bar. Nonetheless they serve the same purpose. We have dozens of them at the house. Everyone here does. My kids know when we go out for a walk, somebody needs to grab a go cup so Dad can put his beer in it. They sometimes even ask for a go cup for their juice!

Locals use these for all sorts of things: they make great paint cups when doing touch-up work, and they are good pen and pencil holders, too. I keep some in the car during Jazz Fest so we can drink a beer on the walk from the car to the gates of the fairgrounds. I'm not alone on this one, not by a long shot.

Go cups provide a nice segue to **Mardi Gras.** If you want a deep dive into Mardi Gras and Carnival, we've talked about it on multiple episodes of the *Beyond Bourbon Street* podcast.

To get you ready, let's cover some of the terms you'll hear when talking about Mardi Gras.

Carnival is the season. It begins on **Twelfth Night,** January 6, also known as the Feast of the Epiphany, and concludes on midnight of Mardi Gras day. The date of Mardi Gras varies based on the date of Easter Sunday, so the length of Carnival can vary.

Mardi Gras is French and means "Fat Tuesday." It is the last day of Carnival.

Parades are put on by Carnival organizations called **krewes.** It is widely believed this spelling and term was coined by the oldest Carnival organization in New Orleans, the Mistick Krewe of Comus, which held its first procession through the city in 1857.

In the days before streetlights, Mardi Gras parades were illuminated by torches known as **flambeaux,** traditionally carried by African-American men who would march alongside the floats and were known to dance and entertain revelers along the way. Many parades continue the tradition today, even though there is plenty of light along the streets and on the floats themselves.

Masked riders toss **throws** to the crowd watching along the route, making Mardi Gras parades simply the best in the world, especially if you are a kid, or young at heart! These throws may include plastic or glass beads, stuffed animals, trinkets, specialty throws with the insignia of the Carnival krewe, including the aforementioned go cups, and doubloons.

Doubloons are coins minted specifically for each organization. On one side will be the name and symbol of the krewe. On the reverse

Flambeaux carriers JAMES CULLEN

Shaka Zulu **JAMES CULLEN**

will be a detailed scene and a description of that year's theme for the parade. Doubloons are usually made of anodized aluminum, though some are made of wood and occasionally collector's versions are made of more precious metals like silver.

The colors of Mardi Gras are purple, green, and gold and were established by **Rex,** which first appeared on the Carnival scene in 1872. *Rex* is French for "king," of course, and the man who reigns as Rex is said to be the King of Carnival. Likewise, his queen is known as the Queen of Carnival. Each year, the mayor of New Orleans ceremoniously hands over the key to the city to Rex, then greets him along the route with a toast of champagne.

The king may reign over the parade and ride on the first float, but the real leader is the **Captain.** He's the chief operating officer. In some krewes, the Captain rides on a horse at the front of the procession. He usually wears an all-white costume and is typically masked.

The place where Mardi Gras floats are housed is called a **den.** Some organizations offer tours: if you are in town and have the chance, this is worth checking out. You can also visit Mardi Gras World along the river. It is both a working art studio and a float den.

The ***boeuf gras,*** or "fatted ox," is another Rex tradition. At one time, an actual ox was included in the parade. These days, a float with a large papier-mâché bull takes its place. You know it's Mardi Gras when you've seen Rex followed by that float with the bull, complete with steam exuding from his nostrils!

King cake is the dessert of Carnival season. It is made of braided Danish pastry dough and is eaten in great quantities during Carnival. Inside the cake is a plastic baby or other small favor. The person who finds the baby inside their piece buys the next cake.

Another important part of Mardi Gras is the **Mardi Gras Indians.** These are tribes (called "gangs" in Mardi Gras parlance) of African-American New Orleanians who wear elaborate hand-sewn suits of beads and feathers. They parade on Mardi Gras morning through the neighborhoods, looking for other gangs in order to see whose Big Chief is the prettiest.

Have you heard the song "Iko Iko"? It's about the Mardi Gras Indians.

OK, enough with Mardi Gras for now.

Let's see, what else can confuse a visitor? **Streetcars.** We do not have trolleys or cable cars in New Orleans—we have streetcars. The St. Charles streetcar line began operation in 1835 and is the oldest continuously running streetcar line in the world.

Today, we're seeing a resurgence in streetcar lines in New Orleans. New lines are being developed all over the city, or so it seems. You'll see both green and red streetcars as you wander around New Orleans.

The green streetcars run on the St. Charles line. The red can be found on the Canal Street and the Riverside lines. You can call them the St. Charles or Canal lines, or you can refer to them by their colors, red or green. Just don't call them trolleys.

Another important difference: the green cars are the older ones. The windows can be opened, but they do not have air-conditioning and they are not wheelchair accessible. The red cars are more modern, have air-conditioning, and are ADA compliant. But the windows don't open.

Let's talk about colors—two in particular that you'll hear locals refer to. Wander through the French Quarter for three minutes and you'll come across shutters painted a deep green. It's got its own name: **French Quarter green.** Go to a paint store in New Orleans, like Helm Paint, and ask for French Quarter green. They'll know how to mix it.

You'll also hear locals refer to **K&B purple.** K&B is a long-defunct local drugstore chain. Their colors included a very distinct purple. Natives still lovingly refer to a certain shade of purple as K&B purple. Don't go to a paint store and ask for this. They might mix it for you, but you won't want to paint anything with it, not unless you want to really stand out!

Another word you'll come across is **pirogue** (PEE-row or PEE-rogue). A pirogue is basically the Cajun version of a canoe. Traditionally made from hollowed cypress logs, today they usually have flat bottoms for easy navigation in the shallow waters of the marsh and swamps, and are often made of wood or fiberglass.

Growing up, we used pirogues to set crawfish nets in shallow water. They are easy to turn over and dump out water and can be carried, which is useful since we would often run into areas that were not navigable in the boat.

You'll also sometimes find them used at a crawfish boil: the boil master will dump a pot of freshly boiled crawfish and vegetables into a pirogue. Guests can then reach in and help themselves!

A **second line** is the line of followers that join in behind the official parade or procession. Today you'll see the second line waving handkerchiefs or twirling small umbrellas. Second lines have their roots in the social aid organizations that were formed after the Civil War to help the newly freed slaves.

These groups often provided basic insurance, loans, and burial needs for their members. They would also hold funeral processions to honor their members. They held parades as a way of introducing the community to their services—a kind of live advertisement, if you will.

Today you can still find second lines in the city as funeral processions, sometimes with a casket and sometimes not. On weekend nights in the French Quarter, you'll see a second line organized as part of a wedding. Guests follow the newly married couple from the site of the ceremony to their reception.

A couple of things define a modern second line: first and foremost, a brass band. They will have some combination of a tuba, trombone, or trumpet, plus a snare or bass drum. Often, you'll see tourists join in behind them, hence creating a second line.

Young trombonist in a second line JAMES CULLEN

While you're following that second line, you might notice our street names. Some are famously difficult to figure out, like **Tchoupitoulas** (CHOP-uh-TOOL-iss) and **Tremé** (tre-MAY). Others are pronounced differently than you would expect.

Here's a brief list to help you out . . .

In the Lower Garden District are streets named for the Muses. We mispronounce nearly all of them, starting with **Calliope:** CAL-e-o. **Melpomene** is MEL-po-mean. **Clio** is not Klee-o, it is Kly-O or CL-10, named after the streetcar line whose destination reads CL-10. **Terpsichore** is TERP-si-core. We don't stop here, though.

You might know **Milan** as the city in Italy. Here, locals pronounce it MY-LAN. **Burgundy** is not like the wine or the region, but rather Bur-GUN-dy. **Marigny** (Mare-i-knee) is *not* Marig-KNEE.

We are also fond of things that aren't around anymore. A local musician named Benny Grunch wrote a song called "Ain't Dere No More" listing many of our favorites. There's even a Facebook group some 40,000 strong by the same name. Some of the more common ones you'll hear us talk about include . . .

Schweggmann's, a local chain of grocery stores that ain't here no more. When people talk about Schweggmann bags, they mean brown paper bags. These were the bags of choice in 1980 when the Saints went 1–15 and the locals called them the Aints. People wore bags over their heads to the football games.

We've mentioned **K&B** earlier, the local drugstore chain with the bright purple and white logo.

Pontchartrain Beach was an amusement park located at the lake at the end of Elysian Fields Boulevard in Gentilly. A couple of miles down the lake in New Orleans East was **Lincoln Beach,** a similar but smaller park for African Americans before desegregation. Both closed long ago, but remnants of each park still remain along the banks of the lake. Work is currently underway to restore the actual beach portion of Pontchartrain Beach. Lincoln Beach was placed on the National Register of Historic Places in 2024. Plans are currently underway to return an amusement facility to the site.

New Orleanians also have our own way of saying things. We don't go to the grocery store to pick up groceries. Instead, we "make groceries." We also are always fixin' to do something, as in about to. If someone says "Let me axe you something," they aren't about to kill you. Instead, they just want to ask you a question. A common greeting is "Where y'at?" The proper response is "I'm good."

Another thing about New Orleans: if someone asks you where you went to school, they mean high school, not college. I've run across this same thing in St. Louis, but not in any other places I can recall. High school pride runs deep here, and those connections can be as powerful as any fraternity or business association.

I was eating lunch one day at Katie's in Midcity with the alumni director of my high school. A guy walked in and sat next to us at the bar. He had a suitcase with him and said he had just come from the airport. He was in town to enjoy Jazz Fest. Over the course of lunch, we chatted with him on and off, and were frequently interrupted by friends. After a while, he looked at us and asked, "Do you know everybody?" Well, the answer was, between the two of us we knew nearly everyone in the place. It helped that the owner was also a graduate of our high school, but this is the way of New Orleans.

I could go on and on, but you've now got an understanding of how we speak about geography. Importantly, you know how to say Tchoupitoulas. You're an expert on lagniappe, and you know why we have parishes. You know what a neutral ground is, and you know not to axe where the trolley stop is.

You know the basics when it comes to food, and you can tell the difference between an étouffée and a jambalaya. You get the whole go cup thing and can't wait to try it out next time you visit. And finally, you know how to answer when someone asks where you went to school.

WHERE TO STAY

The most important thing to know is location matters. Most places you'll want to go in New Orleans are walkable or accessible by streetcar. The few that aren't can typically be reached with a quick rideshare or taxi or bike. The one major exception are the plantations, but we'll discuss those later.

New Orleans is a city that is best experienced by being immersed in it. If you've ever been to Paris and wandered the streets, it is a similar feeling. You want to be able to see, smell, and hear the city. Resist the temptation to hurry from place to place. Instead, challenge yourself to linger, to experience, to observe. This is easier if you choose to stay close to most attractions.

For most people, one of these neighborhoods will be the right choice:

- French Quarter
- Central Business District
- Warehouse/Arts District
- Marigny
- Bywater

THE FRENCH QUARTER

The French Quarter is for you if you like to be in the middle of everything, plan to be out late on Bourbon Street, or simply want the experience of waking up in the original Nouvelle Orleans.

Pros: The original footprint of New Orleans. You can choose from large and small hotels, budget and luxury. You will be steps away from restaurants, bars, museums, and nightlife. From the French Quarter, you can easily enjoy walks along the Mississippi and forays into the Marigny and the Bywater. You can also get rooms with balconies or even a small courtyard at some locations.

Cons: You will be steps away from the noise, smells, and trash left behind by the Bourbon Street warriors who did not use this guide and had one too many hand grenades or hurricanes. During big events, the French Quarter can get very crowded. During Mardi Gras and French Quarter Fest, car traffic is limited, including taxis and rideshares.

RECOMMENDED HOTELS IN THE FRENCH QUARTER

Bienville House (bienvillehouse.com; 320 Decatur St.; 504-529-2345) fits into a wedge of a block a couple of blocks from Canal Street. This

Tiki drinks **MARK BOLOGNA**

80-room hotel is cozy and well appointed. Even many of the standard rooms feature four-poster beds. You're also close to some of my favorite spots, including Cafe Fleur de Lis for breakfast, Irene's or Tujague's for dinner, and the Carousel Bar for drinks. If I have a knock on this property (and it's a small one), some say it can be a bit noisy because of its unique shape. I say that comes with the decision to stay in the French Quarter.

Bourbon Orleans Hotel (bourbonorleans.com; 717 Orleans St.; 800-935-8740) sits just behind Jackson Square and adjacent to one of the busiest sections of Bourbon Street. The courtyard includes a nice pool when you need a break, but make no mistake: you'll be staying here if you want to soak up all Bourbon Street has to offer. Its location does make it a good spot for wandering into the more residential portion of the French Quarter and continuing downriver into the Marigny and Bywater.

The Celestine (thecelestinenola.com; 727 Toulouse St.; 504-332-2200) is a new addition to the French Quarter, but it has already garnered awards. This upscale, 10-room boutique hotel features European styling in a great location.

Holiday Inn–Chateau LeMoyne (ihg.com/holidayinn/hotels/us/en/new-orleans/msycl/hoteldetail; 301 Dauphine St.; 504-581-1303) is a good budget choice in the French Quarter. Rooms are nicer and have more character than you would find in a typical Holiday Inn, and the location is excellent. This is a good spot for a group looking to have fun in New Orleans but save a few dollars on accommodations.

Hotel Monteleone **JAMES CULLEN**

Hotel Mazarin (hotelmazarin.com; 730 Bienville St.; 504-935-8740) is on Bienville, one block off of Bourbon Street. Standard rooms tend to be small, but the furnishings are deluxe and many have a small balcony. Downstairs is the 21st Amendment Bar, which consistently has good live music. The large courtyard offers a nice respite from the craziness of the French Quarter.

Hotel Monteleone (hotelmonteleone.com; 214 Royal St.; 504-523-3341) was opened in 1886 and continues today as a luxury hotel located in the French Quarter one block from Canal Street. The Monteleone is a gorgeous hotel with well-appointed rooms. As an added attraction, the Carousel Bar is located in the lobby.

Hotel Provincial (hotelprovincial.com; 1024 Chartres St.; 504-581-4995) is closer to the French Market than any of the others I've mentioned in this section. This makes it a good location for exploring Ursuline Convent, the Old U.S. Mint, and Esplanade Avenue. It is also convenient for wandering into the Marigny and Bywater. Due to its location, it tends to be quieter than many of the choices closer to Bourbon Street.

Le Richelieu (hotelsone.com/new-orleans-hotels-us/le-richelieu-hotel.html; 1234 Chartres St.; 504-342-4443) offers the same geographic advantages as the Hotel Provincial and recently underwent a renovation.

Maison Dupuy (maisondupuy.com; 1001 Toulouse St.; 800-935-8740) is a small hotel near the back of the French Quarter, which provides some quiet in a manner similar to the Prince Conti. The rooms are fine if not elegant, and many include private balconies. This location provides quick access to Bourbon Street, but it is also just steps away from the Rampart streetcar line and the Tremé. Like most hotels in the French Quarter, the buildings housing the rooms surround a nice courtyard with a pool.

Omni Royal Orleans (omnihotels.com/hotels/new-orleans-royal-orleans; 621 St. Louis St.; 504-529-5333) is a large hotel close to the center of the French Quarter. It is two blocks from Bourbon Street, which provides a bit of a buffer from the noise. It is also close to fine dining at places like Brennan's and Antoine's while being right around the corner from both the Historic New Orleans Collection and the Pharmacy Museum, two places well worth your time.

Prince Conti Hotel (princecontihotel.com; 830 Conti. St.; 888-626-4319) was where my wife and I stayed the night we were married. We chose this hotel because it is in the French Quarter and close to everything while being closer to Rampart Street. As such, it is quieter than those hotels right on or near Bourbon Street.

The standard rooms are small and the carpeted floors may feel a bit dated to some, but it offers a solid value. Some of the suites include a balcony or a private courtyard. Adjacent to the hotel is the Bombay Club, a top choice for drinks and live music.

Sister hotels include the **Place d'Armes, Hotel St. Marie, French Market Inn, and the Lafayette Hotel** located in the Central Business District. All are comparable to the Prince Conti in terms of accommodations, and each offers a unique charm. Links to each of them are available on the Prince Conti website.

The Ritz Carlton (ritzcarlton.com/en/hotels/new-orleans; 921 Canal St.; 504-524-1331) is housed in a building that was once Maison Blanche, a popular department store during the heyday of Canal Street as a shopping destination. As you would expect at the Ritz, accommodations are luxurious, and rooms range from good-sized to very large. There is also a spa and the Jeremy Davenport Lounge, which is a fun place to spend an evening.

Royal Sonesta New Orleans (sonesta.com/us/louisiana/new-orleans/royal-sonesta-new-orleans; 300 Bourbon St.; 504-586-0300) may be for you if you want to be in the middle of it all. This large hotel features lots of amenities including a large pool and courtyard, a high-end restaurant (Restaurant R'evolution), the Desire Oyster Bar, and the Jazz Playhouse. Arnaud's is across the street, and GW Fins is around the corner.

The Westin New Orleans (marriott.com/hotels/travel/msywi-the-westin-new-orleans; 100 Iberville St.; 504-566-7006) may seem like it doesn't fit in this list. It is a large, big-chain hotel. However, it has a few distinctions that made it my hotel of choice in the years when I lived away from New Orleans.

It is situated directly along the Mississippi River. The lobby on the seventh floor features large floor-to-ceiling windows with beautiful views of the river. Request a room with a river view and you'll be treated to the same gorgeous views. The rooms are spacious, and if you are lucky enough to score a corner room on the French Quarter side of the hotel, you'll be treated to watching the sun rise over the river each morning. This is also the place to stay if you are a Marriott Rewards member and have points to use.

CENTRAL BUSINESS DISTRICT

The Central Business District is for you if you want to be close to the French Quarter and one of the hotels fits your profile. As you leave the French Quarter and cross Canal Street, you enter the Central Business District. As the name implies, it contains most of the large business towers, though the Crescent City's business district is fairly compact. Mixed in with businesses are a collection of hotels, apartments, and condos and a smattering of restaurants. Harrah's hotel and casino are located at the end of Canal Street.

Pros: Close to the French Quarter, and easy access to both the Canal Street and St. Charles streetcar lines. A bit quieter than the French Quarter.

Cons: Not as much personality as other spots, and a bit empty at night.

RECOMMENDED HOTELS IN THE CENTRAL BUSINESS DISTRICT

The Eliza Jane (hyatt.com/unbound-collection/en-US/msyub-the-eliza-jane; 315 Magazine St.; 504-882-1234) is part of the Hyatt family of hotels and is very much the close cousin of the Q&C. The name comes from Eliza Jane Nicholson, the first woman publisher of the *Daily Picayune*, a newspaper that was printed on this site.

If you are trying to decide between the Eliza Jane and the Q&C, go with the one whose loyalty program you belong to. The rooms at the Eliza Jane are comfortable, the location is excellent, and the lobby restaurant Couvant is a French brasserie, perfect for a romantic dinner. Family friendly, though no pool.

The Four Seasons (fourseasons.com/neworleans; 2 Canal St.; 504-434-5100) opened in late 2021 and added another high-end, luxury hotel to the area. In addition to the outstanding service and amenities you would expect, the hotel is attached to a new attraction called Vue Orleans, which offers a 360-degree view of the city from its 34th-story observation deck.

Le Pavillon (lepavillon.com; 833 Poydras St.; 504-581-3111) is a beautiful old hotel. It is rumored to have ghosts roaming the upper floor. The lobby and bar have a classic New Orleans feel, and the property is wonderfully decorated for Christmas. They also offer free peanut butter and jelly sandwiches in the evening!

The location may be a shade less desirable than some of the others, but I am picking nits. I have no problem recommending this hotel, which underwent an extensive remodel in 2019. The rooms were updated with a modern

INSIDER TIP: Ask to see or stay in the Napoleon Suite. Rumor has it that Napoleon signed the Louisiana Purchase in a bathtub—the same tub that now resides in this suite at Le Pavillon.

vibe that reminds me of Westin properties. The suites are luxurious, and each has a unique theme. The small rooftop pool is a quiet oasis that will make you forget you are in a business district.

NOPSI Hotel (nopsihotel.com; 317 Baronne St.; 504-962-6500) is named for New Orleans Public Service Inc., which resided in the building years ago and was responsible for electric, gas, and public transportation systems in New Orleans. Today it is a sleek, modern luxury hotel in the Central Business District. It is in a good location near the French Quarter and an easy walk to many museums as well as the Superdome. The lobby bar and poolside rooftop bar are both good spots to enjoy a drink. This property leans towards a younger crowd that enjoys upscale accommodations.

Q&C Hotel Bar (qandc.com; 344 Camp St.; 504-587-9700) is part of Marriott's Autograph Collection. As the name implies, the Q&C has a cozy lobby bar, perfect for taking in happy hour or getting work done. Many rooms feature exposed brick walls and hardwood floors. The hotel is pet friendly and tends towards the hip, younger crowd or the business traveler looking for something smaller than the typical corporate hotel. It is also an excellent choice for the couple who wants a convenient location but doesn't want to be in the French Quarter.

The Roosevelt New Orleans (therooseveltneworleans.com; 130 Roosevelt Way; 504-648-1200) is part of the Waldorf Astoria and Hilton brands. As such, it is an outstanding place to use Hilton points for a stay. The luxurious guest rooms have an old-world charm, and many are quite large.

Originally called the Grunewald, this property has been a hotel since 1893 and was used by Huey P. Long as his de facto New Orleans headquarters. Long's favorite drink was the Ramos Gin Fizz made by Sam Guarino, the head bartender at the Roosevelt. Rumor has it, Long's "deduct box" was kept at the hotel, where he kept "contributions" made by state employees. No one has found the original box, but a replica is now on display in the soaring lobby of the Roosevelt.

The common areas are where the Roosevelt truly shines. From the long main hallway elaborately decorated during the holidays to the Sazerac Bar and Domenica restaurant, you'll be spoiled from the moment you enter. On the roof is a nice small pool, accompanied by a bar.

Selina Catahoula Hotel (selina.com/usa/catahoula-new-orleans; 914 Union St.; 504-603-2442) is around the corner from NOPSI and offers a smaller, more intimate experience that is funky, hip, and eclectic. I discuss the two bars, which I highly recommend, in the chapter on the Central Business District.

The hotel offers a variety of accommodations from standard rooms to small apartments. There is even a community room with bunk beds for a hostel-type experience with the amenities of a hotel. This property is not for everyone, but if funky, eclectic, and adventurous describe you, give it some consideration.

Windsor Court Hotel (thewindsorcourt.com; 300 Gravier St.; 800-262-2662). If the highest standards of luxury are important to you, then this is your spot. This 316-room hotel offers beautiful views of either the river or the city from every room. From the moment you walk in, everything is first-class at this pet-friendly hotel. The common spaces are comfortable, and amenities include a very nice rooftop pool and top-notch spa.

Dining options include the Grill Room for an upscale experience, the Polo Club Lounge for pub fare with drinks, a rooftop bar with light food service, and a first-floor coffeehouse. Le Salon offers a popular British-style tea service on Saturdays and Sundays. The clientele leans older at the Windsor Court, but if you want to be pampered in every way, look no further.

WAREHOUSE/ARTS DISTRICT

This is my favorite spot. It is filled with several hotel choices, is close to the St. Charles streetcar, and is not far from Canal Street. You are near several excellent places to eat and many museums. Plus, you are still within easy walking distance of the French Quarter. The Warehouse/Arts District is for you if you want a great location but don't want the noise of the French Quarter. It is also an excellent area for Mardi Gras parades and smaller festivals held in Lafayette Square. If your interests include the WWII Museum, this is where you want to be.

Pros: Nice selection of hotels, restaurants, and attractions. Close to the French Quarter and not far from the Garden District and Uptown.

Cons: It doesn't have the nonstop activity of the French Quarter, so if that is your interest, this is not the spot for you.

RECOMMENDED HOTELS IN THE WAREHOUSE/ARTS DISTRICT

Drury Plaza Hotel (druryhotels.com/locations/new-orleans-la/drury-plaza-hotel-new-orleans; 820 Poydras St.; 504-529-7800) is the value-driven, pet-friendly choice here, especially if you are on a budget and accommodations are not your primary concern. The rooms are comfortable, though certainly not luxurious. The location is close to restaurants, museums, the St. Charles Avenue streetcar, and the Superdome.

Loews New Orleans Hotel (loewshotels.com/new-orleans; 300 Poydras St.; 504-595-3300) is a large, pet-friendly hotel that feels like a cross between a business traveler's destination and a place that is comfortable for families. Many rooms have views of the nearby river, and the location is close to both the French Quarter and many restaurants and museums. I would recommend it as a consideration for families.

The Old No. 77 Hotel and Chandlery (www.old77hotel.com; 535 Tchoupitoulas St.; 504-527-5271). The Old No. 77 is housed in a building that was built in 1854 and originally used as a coffee warehouse and chandlery. The Warehouse District is so named because for much of New Orleans's history, it was teeming with warehouses. These buildings housed the cargo and goods that arrived and departed from the port of New Orleans, just a couple of blocks away. The immediate area where the Old No. 77 now stands was known as Coffee Row.

Old No. 77 Hotel **MARK BOLOGNA**

While the current address of the hotel is 535 Tchoupitoulas, the name, the Old No. 77, is a nod to the building's heritage. In the early 1900s, New Orleans renumbered its street addresses. Prior to that time, the Old No. 77 building was at 77 Tchoupitoulas.

The hotel is located about three blocks, or a 10-minute walk, from the French Quarter. Rooms feature hardwood floors, exposed brick, and tall ceilings. They focus on connecting with New Orleans, and you'll see that from the artwork in the rooms to the locally influenced products available in the minibar. During my last stay, those offerings included a voodoo doll and locally made rum, along with the usual snacks and drinks.

Rooms range from interior offerings to artist loft suites with carefully curated artwork selected by local artists. There is a free art gallery with rotating exhibits, put together by Where Y'Art. The focus on art continues in the lobby, where visitors can purchase small works of art from a converted cigarette vending machine, now an Art-O-Matic. There is room to work in the lobby and in the chandlery, a small space just off the lobby that also has offerings from local makers.

The Old No. 77 Hotel is home to the award-winning Compère Lapin restaurant. Chef Nina Compton and her partner Larry Miller created a restaurant that blends well with the hotel, and features food that is a mix of Chef Nina's Caribbean roots and the Creole traditions of New Orleans cooking. The bar is front and center and is a great place for happy hour, small plates, and meeting friends.

The Old No. 77 is for you if you like a cool, slightly funky vibe without sacrificing comfort. Yes, the floors creak (they are wood after all), but you won't feel like you are in a road warrior hotel. The location is excellent and provides easy access to the French Quarter, streetcar lines, art galleries and museums, and a range of dining options. This is not your choice if you prefer being right in the mix of everything and are used to the standardized experience of a big-brand hotel.

The Renaissance Arts (marriott.com/hotels/travel/msydt-renaissance-new-orleans-arts-warehouse-district-hotel; 700 Tchoupitoulas St.; 504-613-2330) was one of two places my wife and I would stay when we came to visit in the years we lived away. (The other was the previously mentioned Westin in the French Quarter.)

After the Old No. 77 Hotel, it is my most recommended property in the Warehouse District. They share many characteristics including exposed bricks, a smaller size, and a great location. Unlike the Old No. 77, the Renaissance Arts has a rooftop pool. As an added bonus, the New Orleans Coffee & Beignet Company serves delicious beignets from a window inside the hotel restaurant. No one I ask seems to know this, but I stop in whenever I am close by.

As the name implies, there is a heavy focus on the arts, including an art gallery on the first floor, featuring lots of natural light and a collection of modern art. The common areas are airy and a good place to get some work done or enjoy a book over a cup of coffee.

By Renaissance standards this is a very small hotel. It is only four stories, which makes it useful for another reason: many Mardi Gras parades pass directly in front, so it is easy to dart back to your room for a snack, a quick rest, or a bathroom break. For this reason, a room on the second floor is my favorite, allowing you to run up the steps and avoid the elevators.

The Renaissance Arts is for you if you enjoy a slightly smaller hotel that still offers the consistency and points of the Marriott brand. It is also a great choice during Carnival. This is not your choice if you would prefer to be in the French Quarter or are looking for the least expensive room you can find. As part of the Marriott brand, it also sometimes includes a healthy dose of business travelers and small meetings.

This hotel is showing its age a bit and could use a renovation, but if you are a Marriot Rewards member looking for a smaller hotel, I would choose between the Q&C in the Central Business District and the Renaissance Arts.

MARIGNY & BYWATER

The Marigny and Bywater areas may be a good choice if you have been to New Orleans more than three or four times and want to try a new area. Both of these downriver neighborhoods offer a more eclectic experience. The Marigny is the first neighborhood downriver from the French Quarter as you cross Esplanade Avenue. It is home to Frenchmen Street, which many locals consider the new Bourbon Street for its collection of music venues.

If you continue walking away from the French Quarter through the Marigny, you will arrive in the Bywater. To me, the difference is that the Bywater is more eclectic and artsy. You'll find lots of street art, plenty of corner bars, and good food. Both offer easy access to Crescent Park and excellent views of the city and the river.

Both the Marigny and the Bywater feature smaller hotels, B&Bs, and a plethora of Airbnbs, though residents are not happy about the latter, unless the owner lives on-site. The reason is that investors have purchased whole blocks in some cases, effectively taking away the neighborhood feel.

Pros: Can be quieter than other areas, puts you into a neighborhood, and is a fun area to explore if you've been to New Orleans many times.

Cons: You are farther away from many attractions, and don't have quick access to the St. Charles or Canal Street streetcar lines.

RECOMMENDED HOTELS IN MARIGNY & BYWATER

Hotel Peter and Paul (hotelpeterandpaul.com; 2317 Burgundy St.; 504-356-5200) is in a set of buildings that once comprised a church, a school, a rectory, and a convent. No two rooms are the same, and every one that I've seen has a unique charm to it.

The Rectory houses five guest rooms in addition to the Elysian Bar serving cocktails, coffee, brunch, and dinner. The double parlor is one of my favorite spots for working on the podcast and this book, especially on cold or rainy days.

This hotel is perfect for the traveler who enjoys a hip, upscale experience and wants to be outside of the craziness of the French Quarter. Highly recommend.

Hotel Peter and Paul JAMES CULLEN

Lamothe House Hotel (frenchquarterguesthouses.com; 621 Esplanade Ave.; 504-947-1161) is part of a quartet of small inns, the others being in the French Quarter. Lamothe House sits on the Marigny side of Esplanade Avenue, making it a good location for exploring both the French Quarter as well as the Marigny and the Bywater.

The hotel itself is made up of several buildings including the grand residence, which dates to 1839. In total the property has about three dozen rooms ranging from a smaller but still nice queen room to several large suites. All are well appointed and comfortable. This is a popular choice with *Beyond Bourbon Street* podcast listeners looking for accommodations in a smaller property.

The Mazant (mazant.com; 906 Mazant St.; 504-517-3193) is an 1880s guest house in the heart of the Bywater. Rooms are bright and comfortable; some have private bathrooms, while others share a bathroom off the hallway. The common areas are beautiful.

Chic would be a good word to describe this property. It's perfect for someone wanting to enjoy a different experience, or a group of friends wanting to rent several rooms or the entire house. The property would make a perfect destination for a small wedding.

If there is a downside, you are a healthy walk or a rideshare from the French Quarter and points farther upriver. If your goal is to unwind and hang out in local bars and restaurants in the Bywater and Marigny, this may be the spot for you.

R&B Bed and Breakfast (rbbedandbreakfast.com; 726 Frenchmen St.; 504-943-9500) is fun, funky, and eclectic. It also happens to be on Frenchmen Street, steps away from the live music clubs that make it a popular destination. In the mornings, the area is quiet and perfect for a stroll with a cup of coffee.

The R&B features brightly colored rooms, each with a different theme. The house itself has comfortable areas for sitting, visiting with

R&B Bed and Breakfast **EMILY ROWLANDS**

others, or reading a book. A small side courtyard is perfect for breakfast when the weather is nice. It's not for everyone, but if Frenchmen Street is calling your name and you want to be as close as possible, this is one to consider.

OTHER AREAS

GARDEN DISTRICT

Henry Howard Hotel (henryhowardhotel.com; 2041 Prytania St.; 504-313-1577) is housed in an 1867 mansion designed by the architect of the same name. The 18-room boutique hotel is in the heart of the Garden District and just a block from St. Charles Avenue and the streetcar.

Henry Howard Hotel MARK BOLOGNA

If the focus of your visit is exploring the Garden District and points Uptown, this is an excellent spot. I've recorded a podcast from this property and toured nearly all of the rooms. Some rooms are quite large, the property itself is interesting, and it's a quiet small hotel that I have no problem recommending to you.

TULANE & LOYOLA UNIVERSITIES

Park View Historic Hotel (parkviewguesthouse.com; 7004 St. Charles Ave.; 504-861-7564) is adjacent to Audubon Park. It is perfect if you are visiting a student at Tulane or Loyola, or are making a visit with your child to consider these schools. The home was originally built in 1884 to accommodate visitors to the World International and Cotton Exhibition on the grounds of what is now Audubon Park.

CAESARS SUPERDOME & SMOOTHIE KING CENTER

Any of the hotels in the Central Business District and Warehouse District are within walking distance of the Caesars Superdome and Smoothie King Center. However, the Hyatt Regency and Hyatt House hotels are the closest.

The **Hyatt Regency** (hyatt.com/hyatt-regency/en-US/msyrn-hyatt-regency-new-orleans; 601 Loyola Ave.; 504-561-1234) is a large property with a rooftop pool. **Hyatt House** (hyatt.com/hyatt-house/en-US/msyxd-hyatt-house-new-orleans-downtown; 1250 Poydras St.;

504-648-3118) is its little sister and sits atop an adjoining office building. Hyatt House has a small bar in the large common area that offers nice views of the city and a decent happy hour.

While neither of these properties are on my recommended list for most visitors, they both make excellent places to stay if your main purpose is to attend an event at the Caesars Superdome or the Smoothie King Center.

A NOTE ABOUT SHORT-TERM RENTALS

This is a contentious subject in New Orleans. When short-term rentals came about in a major way, there was no regulation in the city. As a result, investors purchased many properties in the French Quarter, Marigny, and Bywater. In some cases, entire blocks became unofficial hotels. As a result, residents complained their neighborhood culture was disappearing.

Thankfully, the city eliminated short-term rentals in the French Quarter in 2021. There are now some restrictions in other parts of the city, but enforcement is limited.

My advice is if you choose to go the short-term rental route, find a property where the owner lives on-site. You'll have a ready resource of information about the neighborhood and the city, and you'll be helping a resident. Please consider this when making your decision about where to stay.

Henry Howard Hotel guest room MARK BOLOGNA

NEW ORLEANS NEIGHBORHOODS

THE FRENCH QUARTER

The French Quarter is the original footprint of New Orleans. Bounded by the Mississippi River, it extends eight blocks back to Rampart Street. Locals call the area beyond Rampart Street "backatown," as in back of the original city. Standing with your back to the river, the uptown (left) edge is Canal Street, while the downtown side is Esplanade and the street between you and Jackson Square is Decatur. (*Note:* No one here uses compass directions.)

French Quarter door MARK BOLOGNA

Explore early in the morning, and it will be easy to imagine the city at its founding in 1718. There is a hustle and bustle on the uptown side near Canal that gives way to neighborhood life as you cross St. Ann. Here you'll find residents walking their dogs or enjoying a cup of strong coffee while reading the newspaper. Glance up at the iron balconies, where you'll see residents watering plants, reading a book, or playing musical instruments.

Here's how I would do it. Start in Jackson Square, and explore the outer edge first. Notice the Pontalba apartments flanking the square. Said to be the oldest apartments in America, they are the first structures in the city to have the intricate wrought iron New Orleans is known for.

Admire the artwork of the artists who hang their work along the iron fence bordering the square. Stop in front of St. Louis Cathedral and listen to the live music of the street performers. Have your fortune read if that's your thing; if not, step back a bit and simply take in the scene.

Take in mass or a tour of St. Louis Cathedral. A Catholic church has been on this site since the very beginning in 1718. Note the Cabildo and the Presbytère on the left and right sides, respectively, of the cathedral. Part of the Louisiana State Museum System, both are worth visiting depending on your interests. We'll discuss them in greater detail later in this section.

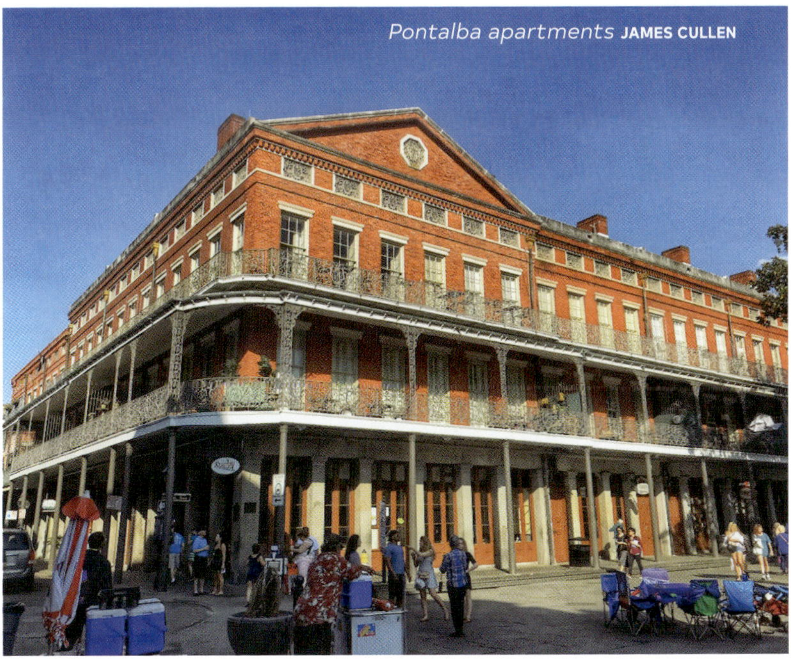
Pontalba apartments **JAMES CULLEN**

Callé D Borbon **JAMES CULLEN**

Be sure to walk into the center of Jackson Square. It's a good place to get photos of the ironwork and the cathedral.

Cross Decatur Street and stroll along the Mississippi riverfront. On your way up the steps, stop at Washington Artillery Park and look back at the cathedral. This is one of the most photographed shots of New Orleans. Continue to the Moonwalk, the boardwalk along the river, and marvel at the ships of all sizes and from ports around the world. It's not hard to imagine this stretch lined with steamships in the early to mid 1800s, stevedores hauling all manner of goods from their decks. Enjoy the sounds of the calliope from the *Natchez* paddle wheeler just upriver.

The daylight hours also allow you to take in the architecture. While it is called the French Quarter due to the city's origins, most of the architecture in the Quarter is actually Spanish. This is primarily due to two fires (1788 and 1794) that destroyed much of the city during Spanish rule. After the second fire, Spanish authorities established building codes prohibiting the building of wooden structures.

A walk through the original footprint in the morning takes you back into the past. When you visit again in the evening, you'll miss the details and be sucked in by the neon lights, the loud house bands, the doorway barkers, and the crowds enjoying their sugary drinks and huge-ass beers. Morning also happens to be the cleanest and quietest part of the day in the French Quarter, so take advantage of it.

Yes, the book and my podcast are called *Beyond Bourbon Street*, but if this is your first visit to New Orleans, you definitely want to at least walk down our most famous street. I prefer to make this walk in the late afternoon. There will be some revelers, but it won't be too crowded—unless there is a special event going on in the city.

I prefer to start at the intersection of Canal and Bourbon Streets and walk straight to the downriver edge at Esplanade Avenue. If you do it this way, you'll immediately be hit with sounds, sights, and smells. Bourbon Street cuts the French Quarter in half, so it provides a good jumping-off point. It also takes you on a walk through time and place, allowing you to see the changes over time and the different uses of different parts of our original city.

In the first block is a pair of very good restaurants, each owned by a different member of the Brennan family: Red Fish Grill and Bourbon House.

Red Fish Grill (redfishgrill.com; 115 Bourbon St.; 504-598-1200) is a casual seafood restaurant serving fresh Gulf seafood and New Orleans classics. They straddle the fence with traditional dishes and inventive takes on classics, such as their flash-fried BBQ oysters served on the half shell. More emphasis is put on preparing fish on the wood-burning grill than frying here.

Red Fish is known for the selection of local fish on its menu and has an excellent raw bar featuring oysters on the half shell. Like its nearby cousin Bourbon House, it is owned by a member of the Brennan family, in this case Ralph Brennan.

Bourbon House (bourbonhouse.com; 144 Bourbon St.; 504-522-0111) puts a big emphasis on their raw oysters and fried seafood platters. If raw oysters aren't your thing, try their BBQ shrimp po-boy. (*Note:* New Orleans BBQ shrimp are not shrimp in BBQ sauce. Instead, the shrimp are sautéed in a mixture of butter, lemon, garlic, and Worcestershire sauce.) Bourbon House is also home to the New Orleans Bourbon Society and features one of the largest whiskey menus in the city.

Felix's Restaurant & Oyster Bar (felixs.com; 739 Iberville St.; 504-522-4440) and **Acme Oyster House** (acmeoyster.com; 724 Iberville St.; 504-522-5973) are across the street from each other on Iberville. Both get lots of well-deserved attention for their raw oysters on the half shell and their charbroiled oysters, but skip the lines and go to Bourbon House or Drago's.

Drago's (dragosrestaurant.com; 2 Poydras St.; 504-584-3911), in the Hilton Riverside, is for you if you desire charbroiled oysters. I don't like the lack of ambience, but the charbroiled oysters more than offset the location in a hotel. If you are visiting relatives in Metairie, go to the original location at 3232 N. Arnoult Road.

Mr. B's Bistro (mrbsbistro.com; 201 Royal St.; 504-523-2078) is where I would go if I had one meal left: Gumbo Ya Ya, BBQ shrimp, a ton of French bread, and a cup of coffee with my dessert. Mr. B's defined the concept of Creole bistro when Cindy Brennan opened this restaurant at the corner of Royal and Iberville in 1979.

BBQ shrimp at Mr. B's Bistro **MARK BOLOGNA**

The gumbo is dark and smoky, and full of bits of andouille sausage and chicken. Their version of BBQ shrimp is traditional in every way. The shrimp come with the heads on, in a sauce made with lots of butter, lemon, garlic, Worcestershire sauce, and pepper. They will take the heads off if you can't stand the sight, but you'll still have to peel the shrimp. Do accept the paper bib they offer, ask for lots of napkins, and wear something dark.

If I could only recommend one restaurant in New Orleans, Mr. B's would be on a very short list of finalists. I am completely biased, but not alone in my opinion. In 1995 Michelle McRaney became the executive chef at Mr. B's. Michelle and her family lived close to Teddy's Grill, my own family's neighborhood restaurant. Her husband and son were frequent visitors while Michelle was manning the kitchen at Mr. B's. We watched their son grow up as he came through the front doors, so our connection is strong. Still, don't let that take away from my recommendation.

Mr. B's is good for lunch or dinner, and has a nice mix of tourists and locals. It's business casual, which in New Orleans means at least decent jeans and a shirt with a collar. You'll see locals wearing jackets at dinnertime, mixed in among the tourists in jeans. Reservations are recommended.

If you are in the mood for debauchery, cross Iberville and take in the sights Bourbon Street often conjures in the minds of visitors. In the next two blocks you'll encounter no fewer than six strip clubs catering to a variety of interests, as well as the infamous Huge Ass Beers. Please skip the Willie's Chicken Shacks. There are a dozen or more terrific places for fried chicken in New Orleans, but this isn't one of them.

You are never far from a more cultured and/or quiet experience. Arnaud's is on Bienville, and Galatoire's is in the block between Iberville and Bienville.

Arnaud's (arnaudsrestaurant.com; 813 Bienville St.; 504-523-5433) is a place to keep in mind for an old-school New Orleans dining experience. Their Reveillon menus are always terrific, plus they have a Mardi Gras museum you can visit while waiting for your food to arrive.

Galatoire's (galatoires.com; 209 Bourbon St.; 504-525-2021) opened in 1905, a full 65 years after Antoine's, yet its menu is similar, with a focus on French Creole classics. Like Antoine's, the food is very good, but regulars don't come here for the best meal they've ever had. They come for the experience, the traditions, the social aspect of it. Especially on Fridays.

For many New Orleanians, Friday lunch means Galatoire's. It consists of a boozy lunch that inevitably turns into dinner, especially on the Friday before Mardi Gras. To experience lunch at Galatoire's, you need to know a few things.

First, they don't take reservations for the downstairs dining room, and you don't want to be anywhere else. Instead, you have two options. One is to stand in the daily queue for reservations (not the entrance to the restaurant). They start assigning tables around 8:30 a.m., but to be assured of a spot at lunch, you'll typically need to be there much earlier, especially on Fridays. The second option, and the one used by locals, is to hire a line sitter. These men and women will hold your place in line and obtain the reservation in your name for a fee.

The only other way in is to be a regular or a VIP, which are often one in the same. Regulars who dine at Galatoire's have their favored servers and tables. They go so regularly, they are expected and are assured a place.

The competition for the Friday before Mardi Gras got so intense, Galatoire's has instead held a reservations auction for many years, with the proceeds going to charity. On days like this, the lunch crowd definitely stays for dinner.

Galatoire's is also one of the last restaurants in the in city to require men wear sports coats at dinner. If you are looking for a memorable experience, Friday lunch at Galatoire's certainly fits the bill. If you are looking for the best meal you've ever had, there are better options.

HISTORIC RESTAURANTS

New Orleans is known for food, but did you know we have 13 restaurants that have been in business for 100 years or more? All have their own stories and specialties, but any of them would be terrific places to include in your exploration of the New Orleans dining scene.

1840: Antoine's
1856: Tujague's
1862: Cafe du Monde
1880: Commander's Palace
1905: Galatoire's
1905: Angelo Brocato's
1906: Central Grocery
1911: Parkway Bakery & Tavern
1913: Pascal's Manale
1914: Napoleon House
1918: Arnaud's
1919: Casamento's
1920: Broussard's

As you resume your trek along Bourbon, you'll be continually barraged by all manner of shops and bars. I prefer to keep walking, maybe with a drink in hand.

On Conti Street, you have two excellent options that could not be more different. Both require you to turn left and head away from the river.

On your right is **Erin Rose** (erinrosebar.com; 811 Conti St.; 504-522-3573), one of the most popular dive bars in the city. You'll find tourists and locals alike enjoying a drink and maybe a po-boy from **Killer Poboys** (killerpoboys.com) in the back. If martinis and live music are more your style, you'll want to try the **Bombay Club** (bombayclub neworleans.com; 830 Conti St.; 504-577-2237) across the street.

Let's go back to Bourbon Street. When you reach St. Louis Street, you again have two very different options. Detour towards the river (to your right) and you'll arrive at Antoine's.

Antoine's (antoines.com; 713 St. Louis St.; 504-581-4422) was opened in 1840 by Antoine Alciatore and is the longest continuously operating family-owned restaurant in the United States. Today, you visit Antoine's for its history, and for the dishes created and/or made famous there, including oysters Rockefeller, eggs Sardou, soufflé potatoes, and baked Alaska for dessert.

The walls of its many rooms are lined with photos of famous guests ranging from royalty to presidents to movie stars, and even a pope. The key is to let your server guide you through the menu, then ask for a tour. You'll be taken through many of the restaurant's themed, historic rooms.

Be sure to ask to see the wine cellar: it's not actually a cellar, but rather a narrow corridor that extends 165 feet deep from Royal Street. When Hurricane Katrina struck in 2005, Antoine's lost 14,000 bottles of wine. The cellar now has a capacity of about 25,000 and is more than half full.

New Orleanians loyal to Antoine's have been visiting for years, and often request their favorite server and table. While it does not have the best food in the city in my opinion, it is a worthy stop, especially for foodies with a love of culinary history.

Note: The **Hermes Bar** at Antoine's is a great place to have a cocktail and order your favorites off the menu if you don't want the more formal experience of dining in the restaurant.

If you decide to continue forward on Bourbon, you come to **Razoo's** (razoo.com; 511 Bourbon St.; 504-522-5100), home of 3-for-1 drinks and loud cover bands. This is a fun place. Yes, it is touristy, but we've had many fun nights reliving the 1980s and '90s while singing loudly and drinking cheap beer.

The next cross street is Toulouse. If you like late night, extremely loud classic rock in very dark, divey bars, then turn right and check out **The Dungeon** (thedungeonneworleans.com; 738 Toulouse St.), but only after midnight. If you are anywhere near my age (54), wear earplugs.

The next few blocks are probably responsible for more regretful decisions than most, because they are home of the sugary high-alcohol drinks. I'm referring, of course, to Pat O'Brien's and Tropical Isle.

Pat O'Brien's (patobriens.com; 718 St. Peter St.; 504-525-4823) is actually located on St. Peter Street, but you can enter from a relatively nondescript entrance on Bourbon. If you prefer the "grander entrance," continue down Bourbon Street a few steps and turn right on St. Peter Street, towards the river and Jackson Square.

INSIDER TIP: Pat O'Brien's has some of the cleanest bathrooms on Bourbon Street. Just be sure to leave a dollar or two for the attendant.

You go to Pat O's for the hurricane and the tradition. Their sugary, from-a-mix hurricanes in the signature glass are fun to say you've had, but don't drink more than one. All that sugar and alcohol is a recipe for a tragic end to your evening and a pounding headache whenever you wake up. Do go, though, and try to sit near the fire pit in the courtyard. It's a fun place, especially during the Sugar Bowl, when college football fans sing their fight songs.

My favorite thing about Pat O'Brien's is the dueling piano bar. Head inside, get a cocktail or a beer, and spend the evening singing along.

Right next door to Pat O'Brien's on St. Louis Street is **Preservation Hall** (preservationhall.com; 726 St. Peter St.; 504-522-2841). If you only do one thing in the French Quarter, a visit to Preservation Hall would be on my very short list of recommendations.

PRESERVATION HALL

Preservation Hall is a must-stop on your musical tour of New Orleans. It has its roots in a 1950s art gallery located at 726 St. Peter Street. Larry Borenstein had opened a gallery there, but found that managing the gallery was cutting into his time to check out the jazz music he loved. To solve the problem, Borenstein started inviting the musicians to "practice" in the gallery.

Keep in mind the time period and the location: 1950s, Jim Crow South. Borenstein couldn't legally host paid performances where blacks and whites mixed. Instead, he allowed these jazz greats to practice in the gallery—and if white friends happened to show up and offer a few dollars, so be it.

In 1960 a couple on their honeymoon decided to pass through New Orleans on their way back to Pennsylvania from Mexico. Allan and Sandra Jaffe ran into a second line in the French Quarter led by Percy Humphrey. Humphrey's band was on their way to Borenstein's art gallery for a jam session.

Allan and Sandra fell in love with the musicians and the scene and soon moved to New Orleans. As the jazz sessions grew, Borenstein handed over daily management of the sessions to the Jaffes. Preservation Hall was formed into what you see today in the early 1960s, complete with the Preservation Hall Jazz Band. Today, as back then, the band performs several shows a night and tours the world to promote traditional jazz.

Preservation Hall **JAMES CULLEN**

Preservation Hall **JAMES CULLEN**

Allan died in 1987, but his son Ben Jaffe leads the band and continues the tradition today, including playing tuba like his father.

Today, Preservation Hall looks much like it has for decades. Patrons sit on the floor, stand, or reserve a spot on a bench. No alcohol or food is served, which makes it a family-friendly environment. There are typically five shows a night, beginning at 5 p.m.

There are two ways to get tickets. The first is to stand in line in advance of the show you want to see and purchase first-come standing room tickets for $25, cash only. The better way to do it is to skip the line and purchase tickets on the Preservation Hall website. General admission is $25, seating is $40, and front row is $50.

For more information about the history of Preservation Hall, check out episode 52 of the *Beyond Bourbon Street* podcast. I interviewed Ben Jaffe: we talked about his parents, the early days of the hall, and how Ben and the band continue the tradition and preservation of jazz through performances and their foundation.

A visit to Preservation Hall is a memorable experience and one that should be on your must-do list. Of note, Preservation Hall allows visitors of all ages.

As you cross St. Peter on Bourbon you come to **The World Famous Cat's Meow** (catskaraoke.com/new-orleans-2; 701 Bourbon St.; 504-523-2951) karaoke bar. I do not do karaoke, but I love this place.

Most people cannot sing well, and drinking alcohol does not improve their abilities. However, every once in a while someone gets on stage at Cat's that belts out a song and the crowd goes wild. If you've ever seen that moment on *America's Got Talent* or a similar show, you know what I'm talking about.

When you cross the next block, Orleans, you get to **Tropical Isle** (tropicalisle.com; 721 Bourbon St.; 504-529-4109). This bar is home of the hand grenade, delivered in a tall plastic replica of a hand grenade attached to a narrow funnel of sorts. The name is appropriate because while it is sweet and not terrible tasting, it does typically cause delayed destruction of your insides. Tropical Isle is a required stop for younger bachelor and bachelorette parties, as well as mid-50s couples who miss their college days.

Take my advice and resist the urge to have both a hurricane and a hand grenade in the same evening.

The more interesting venue in this block is **Fritzel's European Jazz Pub** (fritzelsjazz.com; 733 Bourbon St.; 504-586-4800). Fritzel's bills itself as New Orleans's oldest operating jazz club, and it is one of the few places left on Bourbon Street that consistently delivers. It is small, but always has great live music. It is one of my favorite daytime spots on Bourbon Street.

Fritzel's European Jazz Pub JAMES CULLEN

The next cross street is St. Ann, also known informally as the "lavender line." The French Quarter has been a welcoming place for the LGBTQ community for many years, and the downriver side of the Quarter is informally considered more so than the upriver side.

Bourbon Pub Parade (bourbonpub.com; 801 Bourbon St.; 504-529-2107) and **Oz** (ozneworleans.com; 800 Bourbon St.; 504-593-9491) stand across from each other in this block of Bourbon Street. Oz has long been a favorite spot for late-night dancing, whether you are gay or straight. It is especially "interesting" during Labor Day weekend, when Southern Decadence comes to town.

Note: If you walk down St. Ann half a block towards the river, the headquarters building for *NCIS: New Orleans* is on your left.

INSIDER TIP: Rumor has it there is a speakeasy upstairs at Fritzel's. If you can't figure it out, walk across the street to **Marie Laveau's House of Voodoo** (739 Bourbon St.). They might be able to help.

The other thing that happens as you cross St. Ann is you begin to notice how residential the French Quarter is, particularly on the downriver side and the back side towards Rampart Street.

Beyond Oz, you will find fewer and fewer bars. What you will see are small shops and more residences. This is also why it is worth a walk early in the morning or late afternoon before the sun goes down.

The block between Dumaine and St. Philip Street has three businesses worthy of your attention.

The first is **Cafe Lafitte in Exile** (lafittes.com; 901 Bourbon St.; 504-522-8397), which has been open since 1933 and claims the title of the longest continuously operating gay bar in the United States. The White Horse in Oakland, California, also opened in 1933, but that would be way beyond both New Orleans and Bourbon Street.

Across the street from Lafitte in Exile is **Clover Grill** (clovergrill.com; 900 Bourbon St.; 504-598-1010). It's "only" been open since 1939 but makes up for its relative newness by being open 24 hours a day. They serve great burgers and a basic breakfast, all in a classic diner. The building dates to 1825 and made an appearance in the movie *The Curious Case of Benjamin Button* starring Cate Blanchett and Brad Pitt.

The third must-stop in this block is **Lafitte's Blacksmith Shop Bar** (lafittesblacksmithshop.com; 941 Bourbon St.; 504-593-9761). Lafitte's was built between 1722 and 1732, and is said to be the oldest structure in the United States used as a bar.

Lafitte's Blacksmith Shop JAMES CULLEN

Legend has it that brothers Jean and Pierre Lafitte used the bar as the headquarters for their smuggling and privateering operations throughout much of the 1700s. While it is impossible to certify this as fact, one of the property owners was directly related to Captain René Beluche, who commanded a ship, the *Spy*, in Lafitte's fleet that roamed Barataria Bay, south of New Orleans.

The bar is only lit by candles at night, and you want to order the Frozen VooDoo daiquiri, better known as the "purple drank." It likely contains a combination of bourbon, vodka, Everclear, grape juice, and ice. Have one, but not two.

As you continue on Bourbon Street and cross St. Philip, residences begin to take over. By the time you cross Ursulines in the next block,

Lafitte's Blacksmith **MARK BOLOGNA**

you are essentially reaching the last businesses, and those are a laundromat and a deli that serve the neighborhood.

Don't stop here. By continuing all the way to the downtown side of the French Quarter to Esplanade Avenue, you can appreciate that even Bourbon Street has more to it than what you might've thought prior to your visit.

Once you've navigated Bourbon Street from Canal to Esplanade, you'll have a good sense of the French Quarter. What follows are lists of places worth visiting within the confines of the French Quarter. Where not covered above, I've provided details.

EAT

The French Quarter provides a diversity of foods from New Orleans classics to vegan options.

OYSTERS

Raw and charbroiled oysters are both delicious and popular foods in New Orleans. Go to **Acme Oyster House** (acmeoyster.com; 739 Iberville St.; 504-522-5973), **Felix's Bar** (felixs.com; 724 Iberville St.; 504-522-5973), or **Bourbon House** (bourbonhouse.com; 144 Bourbon St.; 504-274-1808). All three are within half a block of each other, so choose the one with the shorter line. If your party includes guests not partial to oysters, go to Bourbon House.

For charbroiled oysters, visit **Drago's** (dragosrestaurant.com; 2 Poydras St.; 504-584-3911), in the Hilton Riverside.

OLD-SCHOOL FRENCH CREOLE

If classic French Creole dishes in historic dining rooms are your thing, consider a meal at **Antoine's** (antoines.com; 713 St. Louis St.; 504-581-4422), the oldest continuously open family-owned restaurant in the United States. Preorder the baked Alaska, and be sure to ask your server for a tour while your meal is prepared.

Arnaud's (arnaudsrestaurant.com; 813 Bienville St.; 504-523-5433) has the best food of the four restaurants in this section and is also home to a Mardi Gras museum you can tour just by asking.

Galatoire's (galatoires.com; 209 Bourbon St; 504-525-2021) is a favorite among locals, especially for Friday lunches before holidays.

Tujague's (tujaguesrestaurant.com; 429 Decatur St.; 504-525-8676) moved to a new location several years ago, but is well regarded for its history, and its brisket. The grasshopper cocktail was invented here.

Bourbon Street **MARK BOLOGNA**

Galatoire's **MARK BOLOGNA**

UPSCALE DINING

Fine dining is a funny thing. With the exception of Galatoire's, no restaurant in the city requires jackets for men. Most "nice" places are fine with business casual, and some are even OK with jeans and a dress shirt. Call ahead or look online, but if you aren't sure, you can't go wrong with business casual.

The restaurants discussed below are places frequented by locals and visitors. All are excellent choices for a date night or a business meeting. Reservations are always a good idea.

Try Chef Susan Spicer's **Bayona** (bayona.com; 430 Dauphine St.; 504-525-4455) for upscale dining in a 1769 cottage overlooking a beautiful courtyard. You can't go wrong with the specials, especially seafood and duck. Try the garlic ice cream if it is on offer. Vegan and vegetarian friendly.

GW Fins (gwfins.com; 808 Bienville St.; 504-581-3467) is the best upscale seafood restaurant in the city. While there are many excellent places to eat seafood, if a white tablecloth experience is what you want, this is your place.

The Pelican Club (pelicanclub.com; 312 Exchange Place; 504-523-1504) is a great spot for a date night or a client meeting. Feel like an insider when you duck into the picturesque Exchange Alley.

As I mentioned earlier, **Mr. B's Bistro** (mrbsbistro.com; 201 Royal St.; 504-523-2078) is one of my favorite restaurants in New Orleans. I would have my last meal here if I could plan it. A big bowl of chicken and andouille gumbo followed by BBQ shrimp accompanied by plenty of warm French bread. I would top it off with crème brûlée and a cup

Exchange Alley MARK BOLOGNA

of coffee and call it good. Mr. B's is also an excellent spot for a nice lunch. Gumbo and a salad along with that French bread makes for a filling midday meal.

Irene's (irenesnola.com; 529 Bienville St.; 504-529-8811) bills itself as upscale Italian, but I would call it "New Orleans meets Italy." The menu is small but well appointed, with dishes like shrimp and crab pappardelle and duck St. Philip, though less adventurous souls will also find something on the menu just as delicious and well prepared.

Doris Metropolitan (dorismetropolitan.com/new-orleans; 620 Chartres St; 504-267-3500) is a hip steakhouse just off Jackson Square. I had to be dragged into it the first time, but one bite of steak and I was sold. My favorite spot is dining at the bar. Knowledgeable servers, a nice wine list, and great food make this a winner.

Muriel's (muriels.com; 801 Chartres St.; 504-568-1885). Do you believe in ghosts? Want a great meal? This is your place. Casual fine dining, a long history, and a table set for the resident ghost. The menu of seafood, Italian influences, and New Orleans classics is excellent, and it's a great place to keep in mind for Reveillon dinner. Muriel's is located right on Jackson Square, so when the weather's nice, outdoor dining with a view from the balcony is a great choice.

Justine (justinenola.com; 225 Chartres St.; 504-218-8533) is a traditional French brasserie in the heart of the French Quarter, led by Chef Justin Devillier (Le Petit Grocery). Let Justine's neon pink sign welcome you in, where you'll be greeted by a communal dining experience where you can savor French classics. If you desire a bit more intimacy, there are traditional tables as well, though the communal ones are the best way to experience Justine.

BEIGNETS

Fried, pillowy, rectangle-shaped doughnuts showered in powdered sugar are a New Orleans staple. In the French Quarter, check out Cafe du Monde and Cafe Beignet.

Cafe du Monde (cafedumonde.com; 800 Decatur St.; 504-587-0833) has been serving beignets in the French Market since 1862. They are open 24 hours a day, 364 days a year. Christmas Day is the only time they shutter the place. Perfect for all occasions: late night, early morning, with the kids, or on a date.

Cafe Beignet (cafebeignet.com) has several locations in the French Quarter, but the one at 344 Royal Street is my favorite. The interior reminds me of a Parisian cafe. If it is crowded or you just want to be outside, they have a nice courtyard. In either case, the beignets are hot, crispy, and smothered in powdered sugar.

ignets JAMES CULLEN

Cafe du Monde JAMES CULLEN

INSIDER TIP: If there is a line at Cafe du Monde, walk around to the back side of the building and order from the takeout window in Dutch Alley. There you'll find places to sit, or you can walk out to the river just behind you and enjoy the views while you eat your beignets.

fe Beignet MARK BOLOGNA

Cafe Beignet MARK BOLOGNA

BREAKFAST

Breakfast in the French Quarter can range from a cup of café au lait and beignets at Cafe du Monde to the traditional and famous breakfast at Brennan's. If you are visiting for more than a night, make the rounds and enjoy a variety of experiences.

Brennan's (brennansneworleans.com; 417 Royal St.; 504-525-9711). There may be no more famous a place for the morning meal than "breakfast at Brennan's." Certainly a New Orleans tradition, this is the place for an upscale French Creole breakfast. Order the eggs Sardou with a glass of champagne or a brandy milk punch and soak up the ambience.

Brennan's is also a great spot for the younger foodie in your family. It hosts "dining field trips" for area schoolkids, where they learn how to set a table and proper etiquette when dining out.

Cafe Envie (cafeenvie.com; 1241 Decatur St. and 301 Decatur St.) is one of my favorite spots for strong coffee and a light breakfast of pastries or croissants, though they make a good omelette, too. I prefer the location at 1241 Decatur, since you are in the heart of the more residential end of the French Quarter. You'll find residents reading the paper over a cup of coffee, with a dog at their feet. Feel like a local.

Cafe Fleur De Lis (cafefleurdelis .com; 307 Chartres St.; 504-529-9641). If you are looking for a traditional breakfast done well, look no further. You can stick with a traditional omelette, try boudin (a Louisiana sausage made with rice), or have eggs Benedict. This is my French Quarter spot when I want a hearty breakfast prepared with fresh ingredients.

The Ruby Slipper Cafe (theruby slippercafe.net; 204 Decatur St.; 504-525-9355). Don't let the lines scare you away. Put your name on the list or call ahead, then go for a walk. An extensive menu and

Brennan's MARK BOLOGNA

Brennan's side view MARK BOLOGNA

PRALINES

The sugary, nutty delight known as the praline has been a fixture in New Orleans from nearly the beginning. Though no one is certain, it is believed the Ursuline nuns brought the dessert with them from France in about 1727. In France the dessert was made with almonds and sugar, but in New Orleans you'll almost always find it made with pecans, which are grown in the region.

Which is best? A fun way to decide is to visit a handful of the shops below. They are all relatively close to one another. I like to get three or four varieties, grab a cup of café au lait from Cafe du Monde, and head to the riverfront for a taste test.

Aunt Sally's Creole Pralines (auntsallys.com; 810 Decatur St.; 504-524-3373)

Evans Creole Candy Factory (848 Decatur St.; 504-522-7111)

Laura's Candies (laurascandies.com; 331 Chartres St.; 800-992-9699)

Leah's Pralines (leahspralines.com; 714 St. Louis St.; 504-523-5662)

Loretta's Authentic Pralines (lorettaspralines.com; 2101 N. Rampart St.; 504-944-7068)

Magnolia Candy Kitchen (839 Decatur St.; 504-524-2945)

Southern Candymakers (southerncandymakers.com; 334 Decatur St.; 800-344-9773)

large platters of food ensure you'll find something for everyone in your party. This makes it a good spot for families with children.

CASUAL

Buffa's Bar & Restaurant (buffasrestaurant.com; 1001 Esplanade Ave.; 504-949-0038). Billed as the best place you've never heard of, Buffa's could go in several categories. It's part restaurant, part music club, and sits on the border of the French Quarter and the Marigny. The food here is basic, but solid: the usual mix of burgers, wings, po-boys, and pasta dishes you'll find in numerous neighborhood joints throughout New Orleans.

What sets Buffa's apart is the music. It is one of my favorite places to check out live music with a plate of food in front of me. One of my favorite memories is an evening listening to John Boutté and a couple of his seven sisters perform. John is a favorite at Jazz Fest, and an evening with him is like going to church: good for the soul.

Paddle wheeler on the Mississippi
MARK BOLOGNA

Cafe Maspero (cafemaspero.com; 601 Decatur St.; 504-523-6250). With apologies to Central Grocery, Cafe Maspero offers my wife's favorite muffaletta. I think it's because it comes out toasted, which is the way we enjoy muffalettas at home. In any event, Cafe Maspero does a good job with muffalettas and po-boys. My kids love their beignet fries! It's a perfect spot to grab lunch and get off your feet in the French Quarter.

Since I mentioned Central Grocery a moment ago, let's cover it now. Despite Marie's preference, **Central Grocery** (centralgrocery.com; 923 Decatur St.; 504-523-1620) has been offering some of the best muffalettas in town for decades. Head to the back, order your whole or half muffaletta (a quarter of one is a meal for many people), and take it to go. If you are visiting, walk up to the nearby Mississippi River and find a park bench.

INSIDER TIP: Central Grocery muffalettas make a great eat-later, late-night, or on-the-plane-ride-home treat. They wrap them well and will add extra wrapping if you ask. Just be warned the strong smell of olive salad will envelop anyone near you when you open it up. You might have to share!

Napoleon House (napoleonhouse.com; 500 Chartres St.; 504-934-4704). Housed in a building that dates to the early 1800s, the restaurant itself has been in operation on this corner since 1914. Started by the Impastato family, it was purchased by Ralph

Brennan in 2015. When I think of Napoleon House, I think of one thing: their muffaletta, which is served warm, in contrast to Central Grocery. Here, you can sit and bask in an old-world space while enjoying a delicious sandwich along with a cocktail.

Coop's Place (coopsplace.net; 1190 Decatur St.; 504-525-9053). A favorite of our Beyond Bourbon Street Facebook Krewe (facebook.com/groups/BeyondBourbonStKrewe), visitors and locals enjoy Coop's for its laid-back atmosphere, fried chicken, and casual New Orleans basics. Not for the foodie, Coop's is a solid place for an easy lunch or dinner, along with a few drinks. It also has the advantage of being on the "quieter side" of the French Quarter.

The Gumbo Shop (gumboshop.com; 630 St. Peter St.; 504-525-1486). Popular with locals and visitors, the Gumbo Shop is frequently on my go-to list when asked for a recommendation. While nothing jumps out at me as the "best of," it is a place where you can get a very good version of classic New Orleans dishes. Chicken and sausage gumbo? Jambalaya? Red beans and rice? Shrimp Creole? Crawfish étouffée? Check. Check. Check. Check. Check. You get the picture.

Additionally, I love the space. You enter through an alley and are transported back in time to the early 1800s.

For many years my family would attend Christmas Eve Mass at St. Louis Cathedral just down the street. After Communion my role was to sneak out (sorry, Father!) and run down the street to secure a place in line at the Gumbo Shop before the crowds came as Mass let out. Once assembled, we would enjoy a Reveillon dinner before heading home to await St. Nick. The Gumbo Shop's Reveillon dinner is one of the least expensive in town and includes café brûlot, an old drink served at only a few old-line New Orleans restaurants.

Café brûlot translates to "burnt brandy" and starts with a strong coffee to which brandy and other liquors are added. The brandy is set aflame just before the server ladles each serving into cups.

PO-BOYS

Several of the above-mentioned restaurants serve excellent po-boys. I grouped these three together because they allow you a range of experiences. Pick the one that matches your style the best and enjoy.

Johnny's Po-Boys (johnnys-po-boys.res-menu.com; 511 St. Louis St; 504-524-8129) is a solid choice for a po-boy in the French Quarter. No frills, this cash-only place has red-and-white-checkered plastic tablecloths on the tables and screams neighborhood dive. Don't be fooled. The sandwiches are good and reasonably priced. Johnny's has been around forever, with good reason.

Mahony's Po-Boys (mahonyspoboys.com; 901 Iberville St.; 504-717-2422). Award-winning po-boys plus comfort food make this an excellent destination after a morning of exploring the French Quarter. Daily lunch specials are always a good bet, as are the seafood po-boys.

INSIDER TIP: The stand-alone shop called Big Killer Poboys is fine, but the original pop-up in the back of Erin Rose bar is my favorite of the two locations. You get all the atmosphere of Erin Rose (more on that later) as well as the uniqueness of the Killer Poboy experience.

Killer Poboys (killerpoboys.com; 219 Dauphine St. and 811 Conti St. in Erin Rose; 504-462-2731). If Johnny's is old school, Killer Poboys is what happens when you apply a modern take to a tradition. Roasted sweet potato, BBQ chicken confit, and glazed pork belly are a few of the offerings on this unique po-boy menu. Good spot for vegetarians who want a po-boy.

DIVES YOU DON'T WANT TO MISS

Verti Marte (vertimartenola.com; 1201 Royal St; 504-525-4567). This 24/7 market and deli serves very good sandwiches when you need some nourishment after a long night.

Port of Call (portofcallnola.com; 838 Esplanade Ave.; 504-523-0120). Self-billed as the best burger in New Orleans, Port of Call is my favorite dive place to have a meal and a drink. Their burgers are indeed very good and come with a stuffed baked potato. The thing that makes Port of Call special is the burgers plus the drinks. With names like Monsoon and Huma Huma (my favorite), they are served in tall plastic cups and are very strong. This place is popular with locals and tourists, so go during off-hours for the shortest wait. Sit at the bar if you can and enjoy the conversation with their terrific bartenders.

Port of Call JAMES CULLEN

DRINK

I covered Bourbon Street earlier, but there are far better places to imbibe in the French Quarter once you leave the neon lights and doorway hawkers behind.

Carousel Bar (hotelmonteleone.com/entertainment/carousel-bar; 214 Royal St.; 504-523-3341) has an actual carousel as its primary bar. Go during off-peak hours for your best shot at sitting at the bar. They also often feature live music. Popular with locals and tourists, it is a great place to enjoy a classic New Orleans cocktail. If you're lucky, Marvin will be behind the bar. If so, be sure to order a Sazerac.

Jeremy Davenport is one of the best trumpeters and entertainers in the city. If old-school jazz is your style, be sure to take in the swanky confines of the **Davenport Lounge** (ritzcarlton.com/en/hotels/new-orleans/dining/davenport-lounge; 921 Canal St.; 504-524-1331) inside the Ritz hotel.

The Bombay Club (bombayclubneworleans.com; 830 Conti St.; 504-577-2237) is the place for a martini in a cozy environment with live jazz music. Attached to the Prince Conti Hotel, it feels a bit like a speakeasy with its spot off the street. I feel like I am slipping back in time, and so will you.

Decidedly more casual than the listings above, the **21st Amendment Bar** (21stamendmentlalouisiane.com; 725 Iberville St.; 504-378-7330) is one of my favorites because of its live music. This small space is always bustling, yet seems to be unknown to many locals. Don't let that deter you.

If tiki drinks are your jam, you'll want to stop in at **Beachbum Berry's Latitude 29** (latitude29nola.com; 321 N. Peters St.; 504-609-3811). Just steps off Bourbon Street, you are transported to Polynesia. A great place to get out of the heat, crowds, and noise.

Erin Rose (erinrosebar.com; 811 Conti St.; 504-522-3573) is just steps from Bourbon Street but feels a world away. A mix of regulars and tourists, drink prices are much cheaper than the nearby tourist places and it feels like a neighborhood bar because it is. Popular with service industry workers, it is a wonderful spot to take a break from the neon lights or to while away an afternoon. The original Killer Poboys started here and still operates a spot from the back of the bar in case you get hungry.

Manolito (manolitonola.com; 508 Dumaine St.; 504-603-2740) is a tiny bar named after Manuel "Manolito" Carbajo Aguiar, who enjoyed a longtime tenure at the El Floridita bar in Havana. Their specialty is the hand-blended daiquiri. They also have small, but very good, menu of Cuban-inspired dishes.

Jewel of the South (jewelnola.com; 1026 St. Louis St.; 504-265-8816) has received numerous awards, including being named as one of the 50 best bars in the world. An excellent place for a craft cocktail, a glass of wine, and/or dinner.

The Will & The Way (thewillandtheway.com; 719 Toulouse St.; 504-354-1139) was designed to feel like a lobby for the neighborhood's locals—lots of nooks and crannies to hang out in. First-class cocktails and upscale pub food.

SEE & DO

You could spend several days exploring the French Quarter. A good place to start is the Louisiana State Museum. Of the nine museums that make up the system, five reside in the French Quarter. For our purposes, let's start with the Cabildo and the Presbytère. Flanking St. Louis Cathedral and facing Jackson Square, they both have a unique focus.

The **Cabildo** (louisianastatemuseum.org/museum/cabildo; 701 Chartres St.; 504-568-8975), on the left side of the cathedral as you face it, was built between 1788 and 1795 after the first of the great fires in New Orleans. It was the seat of Spanish government and site of the transfer ceremony of the Louisiana Purchase in 1803.

Today the Cabildo focuses on the history of Louisiana and New Orleans. Permanent exhibits include the Battle of New Orleans, Napoleon's death mask, and an exhibit titled *We Love You, New Orleans!*

The Cabildo MARK BOLOGNA

The Presbytère **MARK BOLOGNA**

The **Presbytère** (louisianastatemuseum.org/museum/presbytere; 751 Chartres St.; 504-568-6968) sits on the downriver side of the cathedral, across the street from Muriel's. Two permanent exhibits tell different parts of New Orleans history. *Mardi Gras: It's Carnival Time in Louisiana* covers the different traditions of our favorite holiday. It also includes floats kids young and old can climb on! *Living with Hurricanes: Katrina and Beyond* tells the story of Hurricane Katrina and its aftermath, as well as the recovery and rebuilding efforts. A sobering exhibit but well worth the time.

St. Louis Cathedral (stlouiscathedral.org; 615 Pere Antoine Alley; 504-525-9585) is one of our most recognizable landmarks. If you've seen a picture of Jackson Square, you've seen the cathedral with its triple steeples. This site has been home to a Catholic church since 1727. Masses are open to everyone, and tours are available.

St. Louis Cathedral **MARK BOLOGNA**

Next up are two spots many visitors overlook. You should not.

A couple of blocks behind the cathedral is **Madame John's Legacy** (louisianastatemuseum.org/museum/madame-johns-legacy; 632 Dumaine St.; 504-568-6968), another part of the Louisiana State Museum system. Located on Dumaine Street between Chartres and Royal, it offers free admission.

Madame John's Legacy **MARK BOLOGNA**

The building is one of the oldest residences in the French Quarter, dating to 1788. The original structure on the site where Madame John's now sits was one of many destroyed in the 1788 fire. At the time, the house on this property was owned by Manuel de Lanzos, a captain in the Spanish military. He lived in the home with his wife, Gertrudis, and their six daughters. As an officer, Captain Lanzos would have been an influential member of New Orleans society. As such, he was able to find a contractor and make plans to rebuild the home within days after the fire.

Unfortunately, New Orleans suffered a second great fire in 1794, wiping out nearly 300 buildings. The Lanzos home somehow survived that fire and today is the only house in the French Quarter that is similar to what you would've seen before 1788. What follows is a quick walk-through, but it will help you gain a sense of what a home was like at the time.

It is a raised French Colonial–style home. You'll note the raised galleries, which provided additional living space and allowed for better air movement. The double doors, common in much of New Orleans architecture, also helped with airflow. Finally, the home is raised, in part to alleviate the risk of flooding. Interestingly, after Hurricane Katrina many homes throughout New Orleans are once again built on piers.

There are no furnishings in the home today. Instead, the focus of the museum beyond the architecture is a collection of Newcomb pottery. The pottery gets its name from the women's college at Tulane University. More specifically, the college had a pottery program from 1895 to 1940 that focused on the Arts and Crafts style. It is believed more than 70,000 pieces of art were produced over the 45-year life of the program. The pottery remains popular today.

Madame John's Legacy is definitely worth a quick stop, especially if you visit during warmer weather and need a break from the sun. The property is currently undergoing restoration as I type this in 2025, so be sure to call ahead to see if it is open.

Do visit the **Historic New Orleans Collection** (hnoc.org; 520 Royal St.; 504-523-4662). Composed of three campuses all close by, you'll start at 520 Royal Street. HNOC is not only a museum but also a research center and a publisher. If there is a piece of New Orleans history you wish to study in detail, the library at HNOC is a good place to start.

Historic New Orleans Collection **MARK BOLOGNA**

Exhibits rotate regularly and are complemented by permanent galleries highlighting Louisiana history and life in the French Quarter. Admission is free. This is another great spot to get out of the sun, and to spend an hour or more wandering the exhibits. HNOC also has a robust online presence (hnoc.org/exhibitions/virtual-exhibitions) that expanded greatly in 2020 in response to COVID.

The **New Orleans Jazz Museum** (nolajazzmuseum.org; 400 Esplanade Ave.; 504-568-6993) resides in what locals call the Old U.S. Mint. Part of the Louisiana State Museum system today, it houses an ever-changing set of exhibits. What draws me in is the immersive aspect, with listening stations, a recording studio, instruments, and a steady schedule of live music performances.

Check out Louis Armstrong's trumpet and Fats Domino's piano. There is also an exhibit about the building's life as a mint. It is the only mint in the United States that produced both Union and Confederate currencies, though obviously not at the same time.

There is free live music every day except Monday. The Jazz Museum is a good place to go just before lunch, then head over to Port of Call or Buffa's. Both are on Esplanade just a few blocks from here.

The **New Orleans Jazz National Historical Park** (nps.gov/jazz; 916 N. Peters St.; 504-504-589-4841) often gets confused with the New Orleans Jazz Museum, but they are two different entities. The park is part of the National Park Service and is near the end of Dutch Alley, just off Decatur Street. Enjoy free live music and other performances that tell the story of jazz history and culture in New Orleans.

The Catholic Church and the Ursuline nuns have played a role in New Orleans from its earliest days. A visit to the **Old Ursuline Convent Museum** (oldursulineconventmuseum.com; 1100 Chartres St.; 504-529-3040) is definitely worth your time and a stop many people overlook. The convent was designed in 1745 and is the oldest building in the Mississippi River Valley.

Did you know the first licensed pharmacist in America was New Orleans–born Louis J. Dufilho Jr.? His apothecary was the first sanctioned one in the country and was located at 514 Chartres Street. It is now the site of the **New Orleans Pharmacy Museum** (pharmacy museum.org; 504-565-8027). Explore this small museum and learn about Dufilho as well as Antoine Peychaud—you might recognize that name because of Peychaud's Bitters. These bitters are used in the Sazerac, a drink invented in New Orleans.

Spend some time on Royal Street and check out the many art galleries and antiques shops. My favorite and one of the largest is **M.S. Rau** (rauantiques.com; 622 Royal St.; 888-557-2406). Rau often has

New Orleans Pharmacy Museum **MARK BOLOGNA**

paintings by masters like Monet, Manet, and Renoir, as well as incredible antiques, jewelry, and more. For most of us, it is a wonderful window-shopping experience. If you are in the market for high-end antiques, it is definitely worth a stop.

Royal Street is also home to numerous street musicians. They are transient in nature, but often the same groups will occupy the same corner for many years if they are successful. Definitely seek out Doreen Ketchens and her family.

Doreen Ketchens is a classically trained clarinet player who performs traditional jazz with her family at the corner of Royal and St. Peter Streets. I grew up playing clarinet (poorly) so I may be biased, but I can easily spend an afternoon listening to Doreen play. She has performed around the world: don't miss the opportunity to hear her play in New Orleans.

The **LaLaurie Mansion** (1138 Royal St.) is not open for tours but is worth knowing about. In 1832 the home construction was finished, and Madame Marie Delphine McCarty LaLaurie and her third husband moved in. While Madame LaLaurie was well-known in social circles, rumors circulated that she was abusive to her slaves. In fact, she was called to court at least once for her behavior, indicating it must have been quite excessive.

In March 1834 the LaLauries were hosting a party when a fire broke out. Concerned neighbors rushed to the scene to help, but were met with resistance. When they finally were allowed to enter, they encountered a ghastly scene. They found slaves chained to walls. Others had been mutilated and/or subjected to medical experiments.

The LaLauries fled New Orleans and were never prosecuted. Today, the mansion is part of many ghost tours in New Orleans, though they are often filled with inaccuracies about both the structure of the mansion and the events that transpired.

The most authoritative source about Madame LaLaurie is the excellent book by Carolyn Morrow Long, *Madame LaLaurie, Mistress of the Haunted Mansion*. I interviewed Carolyn on the *Beyond Bourbon Street* podcast in episode 74.

If haunted history is your thing, there are two tour companies I recommend. The first is **New Orleans Haunted Ghost Tours** by Jonathan Weiss (jonathanweisstours.com). Jonathan offers a variety of tours including the French Quarter and Frenchmen Street, as well as a Voodoo Tour.

Next up is **Orion Couling** (orioncoulingnola.com). A previous guest on the podcast and an incredible storyteller, Orion is constantly researching to improve his tours.

Looking for a kid-friendly activity in the French Quarter? You'll want to check out both the **Audubon Aquarium of the Americas** (audubonnatureinstitute.org/aquarium; 1 Canal St.; 504-565-3033) and the **Audubon Butterfly Garden and Insectarium** (audubonnatureinstitute.org/insectarium; 1 Canal St.; 504-861-2537). Both are part of the Audubon Institute, as is the zoo. If you have a large family or think you might go to two or three of these, consider a one-year membership.

CENTRAL BUSINESS DISTRICT & WAREHOUSE/ARTS DISTRICT

Ironwork and ferns **MARK BOLOGNA**

The Central Business District (CBD) starts as you leave the French Quarter and cross Canal Street. It is bounded by the Mississippi River on your left and Claiborne Avenue approximately one mile to your right. It continues until you cross Poydras Street a couple of blocks where it blends into the Warehouse/Arts District (which I'll now refer to as the Warehouse District). This area continues until you reach the I-10 overpass.

Here you'll find the white-collar corridor of New Orleans: banks, office buildings, and the federal courthouse. For our purposes, you'll also find a nice collection of hotels and, as you head into the Warehouse District, museums, restaurants, and art galleries.

As a place to stay, this area is my favorite. Nice hotels can be found only a few blocks from the French Quarter, but far enough away to escape the noise and the lights when you are done for the evening. The CBD/Warehouse District also puts you in a central location with easy access to both major streetcar lines, the aforementioned museums, and the French Quarter.

Canal Street streetcar **MARK BOLOGNA**

This area also includes the Caesars Superdome and the Smoothie King Center, its smaller sibling. The Superdome is home to the New Orleans Saints and other large events, while Smoothie King hosts the New Orleans Pelicans basketball club as well as a full schedule of music concerts throughout the year.

Against the riverside edge of this area, you'll find the Riverwalk and the Ernest N. Morial Convention Center. The Riverwalk presently houses a collection of outlet shops, while the Morial Convention Center hosts the largest conventions that come to New Orleans. Both sit on land that was in the heart of the 1984 World's Fair.

Drago's (dragosrestaurant.com; 2 Poydras St.; 504-594-3911), located in the Hilton Riverside Hotel, is the place to go for chargrilled oysters. While the ambience is lacking, the food is not.

Restaurant August (restaurantaugust.com; 301 Tchoupitoulas St.; 504-299-9777) is an upscale (and expensive) French Creole destination featuring a Louisiana-based menu including fresh local fish, duck, and oysters. If you are looking for an intimate dining experience for a special occasion, August may be your place. Reservations required.

Couvant (couvant.com; 317 Magazine St.; 504-324-5400), in the Eliza Jane hotel, is a traditional French brasserie. Slightly upscale, this is a nice spot for a business lunch or date night.

Luke (lukeneworleans.com; 333 St. Charles Ave.; 504-378-2840) is a charming combination Creole French brasserie featuring a raw bar, fresh Louisiana ingredients, and French classics. I particularly like Luke for a nice lunch when you want something more than a po-boy.

Commerce Restaurant (commercerest.com; 300 Camp St.; 504-561-9239) is a positively old-school simple corner restaurant perfect for a classic breakfast and a good spot with the kids. You'll be surrounded by both blue-collar and white-collar workers who know what a good value it is.

As you cross Poydras Street with the French Quarter behind you, the line between the Central Business District and the Warehouse District starts to blur.

Compère Lapin (comperelapin.com; 535 Tchoupitoulas St.; 504-599-2119) is a mix of Caribbean and Creole influences. Led by Chef Nina Compton, Compère Lapin is located inside the Old No. 77 Hotel and Chandlery, one of my top hotel recommendations outside the French Quarter. This spot is also one of my favorite places for well-made cocktails. Reservations recommended.

St. James Cheese Company (stjamescheese.com; 641 Tchoupitoulas St.; 504-304-1485) is a good spot for a light lunch if you've been wandering through the nearby art galleries and museums. Sandwiches, soup specials, and the ploughman's lunch are all good choices. If gumbo is on offer, be sure to order it.

La Boca (labocanola.com; 870 Tchoupitoulas St.; 504-525-8205), an Argentinean steakhouse, is several blocks farther along Tchoupitoulas Street. Don't think of waiters carrying skewers of meat—that's a Brazilian-style steakhouse. Instead, La Boca claims to offer the largest selection of steak cuts in New Orleans. I tend to agree.

In addition to great steaks and the accompanying sauces, their empanadas are tasty, as are the desserts. The wine list is 100 percent Argentinean as well, so if you love Malbecs, this is your place. Reservations recommended. *Note:* It *is* a steakhouse, so not the place if members of your party are vegan or vegetarian.

Cochon (cochonrestaurant.com; 930 Tchoupitoulas St.; 504-588-2123) is Donald Link's traditional Cajun restaurant. Cajun refers to the Acadiana region of Louisiana some 140 miles to the west, and is not as common as you might think in New Orleans. As the name implies, this restaurant is focused on pork, but does nod to its Louisiana roots with several fish dishes typically on the menu. The crawfish pie and the fried boudin are both excellent starters. The Louisiana Cochon is the daily pork special and is the choice if you've been lured by the name. Reservations recommended.

For lunch, try **Cochon Butcher** (cochonbutcher.com; 930 Tchoupitoulas St.; 504-588-7675), the more casual sibling of Cochon. With its large selection of sandwiches and small plates, Cochon Butcher offers something for everyone. Very close to the Morial Convention Center if you are attending a conference and want something better than what's on offer in the center.

Emeril's (emerilsrestaurant.com; 800 Tchoupitoulas St.; 504-528-9393) is well-known and still excellent. It recently underwent a renovation and an overhaul of its menu that has been well received.

Pêche Seafood Grill (pecherestaurant.com; 800 Magazine St.; 504-522-1744), as the name implies, is the place to go if you like Louisiana grilled fish. Like Cochon and Herbsaint, Pêche is a creation of Chef Donald Link. Reservations recommended.

Herbsaint (herbsaint.com; 701 St. Charles Ave.; 504-524-4114) is yet another of Donald Link's restaurants. This one is in an intimate space, with a small menu made up of locally sourced ingredients. Heavy on fish and duck, the menu also includes steak and chicken dishes. The gumbo is excellent. A good place for date night. Reservations recommended.

Desi Vega's Steakhouse (desivegasteaks.com; 628 St. Charles Ave.; 504-523-7600). This upscale, classic steakhouse features a variety of cuts. In addition to the excellent food, Desi Vega sits on the edge of Lafayette Square. The bright dining room is a good spot for the after-work crowd as well as pre-concert or before a Saints game.

Ugly Dog Saloon (theuglydogsaloon.com; 401 Andrew Higgins Blvd.; 504-569-8459) is another good lunch spot not far from the convention center. The Ugly Dog features burgers and BBQ, both of which are better than expected given the unassuming looks of the place from the outside.

Closer to the Superdome is **Willa Jean** (willajean.com; 611 O'Keefe Ave.; 504-509-7334). This James Beard Award winner is a nice place for brunch or lunch with friends. I particularly love the rich-tasting BBQ shrimp and grits. They also offer an assortment of pastries if you are on the go, as well as their well-known biscuits. Reservations recommended for brunch.

DRINK

The Roosevelt Hotel's **Sazerac Bar** (therooseveltneworleans.com/dining; 130 Roosevelt Way; 504-648-1200) is the first place that comes to mind. The Sazerac was created in this iconic bar and is considered by many to be the first mixed drink. The bar was a favorite of Huey P. Long, who favored the Ramos Gin Fizz and made the Roosevelt his informal New Orleans office while serving as governor of Louisiana.

Stepping into the Sazerac is like stepping back in time. From its dark wood walls to its clubby chairs and murals, there are few places better suited for an evening of cocktails. The Roosevelt itself is a grand hotel whose lobby is spectacularly decorated during the Christmas holidays. The Sazerac's location only a few blocks from the Saenger Theatre makes it a popular place for pre-performance cocktails.

At the **Selina Catahoula Hotel** (catahoulahotel.com; 914 Union St.; 504-603-2442), you'll find two bars worth visiting. In the hotel lobby is the **Pisco Bar.** The bartenders are excellent, and the wide range of pisco drinks make for an interesting cocktail hour. They also have a list of little-known historic cocktails they mix, but be forewarned: many concoctions from yesteryear sound better than they taste! This is not a slight in any way on the bartenders, but rather on the recipes themselves.

The Catahoula's Pisco Bar **MARK BOLOGNA**

Head upstairs to the **Rooftop Bar** for a hidden gem. The views are good if not spectacular, but the coziness and thoughtfulness of the space make it great for

The Catahoula's Rooftop Bar MARK BOLOGNA

conversation or an intimate drink with someone special. The menu is different than in the Pisco Bar, and features local craft beers as well as wines from Central America and Spain. I like the spot so much, I've even recorded a podcast episode up there!

The **NOPSI Hotel** (nopsihotel.com; 317 Baronne St.; 504-962-1463), across the street from the Selina Catahoula Hotel, similarly offers a lobby bar and a rooftop bar. **Henry's Gin Bar** in the lobby is an ode to Henry C. Ramos, creator of the Ramos Gin Fizz and owner of the Imperial Cabinet Saloon, which was located a block from the present-day location of the NOPSI Hotel. I enjoy sitting in this lobby bar drinking a well-made old-fashioned and visiting with the bartenders. There is often a jazz band playing nearby.

Above the Grid is the hotel's poolside rooftop bar. While I do not like the space as much as the Catahoula's Rooftop Bar, it does offer nice views of Downtown and is worth a walk up there if you are already in the building.

SEE & DO

The Central Business/Warehouse District is a place to focus on museums and art galleries. In terms of art galleries, you'll want to wander Julia Street. Let's talk about museums and other places to stop and explore.

The National WWII Museum (nationalww2museum.org; 945 Magazine St.; 504-528-1944) is at the top of the list. Consistently voted the number-one attraction in New Orleans, the museum focuses on the American experience during WWII, both home and abroad.

This is a large museum that can take up anywhere from half a day to two full days depending on your interest. There is much to explore. For a detailed look into the museum, check out episode 70 of my podcast.

The **Ogden Museum of Southern Art** (ogdenmuseum.org; 925 Camp St.; 504-539-9650) offers an ever-changing series of exhibitions as well as the largest permanent collection of Southern art. Collections include a focus on visual art, as well as music, literature, and even the culinary history of the South. The Ogden offers a variety of educational experiences for children and adults, including artist workshops and Art Talks.

The **Confederate Museum** (confederatemuseum.com; 929 Camp St.; 504-523-4522) is the oldest museum in Louisiana and houses one of the largest collections of Confederate artifacts. Opened in 1891, I have mixed feelings about it. In the shadow of the now-removed monument to Robert E. Lee, the Civil War was clearly fought from the Confederate perspective to defend slavery. At the same time, the museum does document this terrible time in the history of the United States and is thought-provoking, especially with its juxtaposition to the nearby WWII Museum. While not a must-stop, it is well done and worth your consideration.

The **Contemporary Arts Center** (cacno.org; 900 Camp St.; 504-528-3805) is known to locals as the CAC. The CAC bills itself as a multidisciplinary arts center supporting contemporary art and new art forms. The space itself is visually stunning, with large light-filled galleries. The changing exhibits feature artists not only from New Orleans but from all over the world. The CAC hosts a variety of events and is a favorite of locals.

The **American Italian Cultural Center** (aiccnola.org; 537 S. Peters St.; 504-522-7294) honors and celebrates Italian culture in Louisiana. There is a small museum as well as lectures and classes in speaking Italian. Across the street is the **Piazza d'Italia,** an urban plaza dedicated to the large Italian immigrant population that came to New Orleans in the late 1800s and early 1900s.

Mardi Gras World (mardigrasworld.com; 1380 Port of New Orleans Place; 504-361-7821) offers a behind-the-scenes look at Mardi Gras parades. You'll not only see actual parade floats stored in the large den, but learn about the planning and artistry that goes into these unique works of art. If you visit New Orleans during Mardi Gras, skip this museum. If you are here any other time of the year and have never been to Carnival, consider putting this one on your list.

The Sazerac House (sazerachouse.com; 101 Magazine St.; 504-910-0100) offers complimentary tours, tastings, and exhibits that cover the history of this original New Orleans concoction. Among my favorite exhibits is the virtual cafe where local chef Kevin Belton is joined by podcaster Poppy Tooker. You sit at a cafe stool and "order" from a virtual menu. Based on your selection, Kevin and Poppy appear on-screen and prepare your food or drink selection along with a description and history. It's really well done and a fun way to learn about classic New Orleans foods and cocktails.

Sazerac is part of the Buffalo Trace Distillery brand. As such, the gift shop offers a wide selection of their spirits and often sells some of their most limited offerings. Admission is free.

Vue Orleans (vueorleans.com; 2 Canal St.; 504-285-3600) is located adjacent to the Four Seasons Hotel and features interactive exhibits about New Orleans history as well as a 360-degree view of the city from the 34th-floor observation deck.

As you enter the space, you are greeted by large screens and a wall. The screens allow you to select a historical character who then "comes to life" and tells you about themselves and their New Orleans. They are amazingly lifelike. The wall is sort of a combination timeline and mural depicting famous New Orleans events, activities, food, etc. You wave your hand over an area and are treated to a description of the item or event.

The sweeping views from the observation deck are the best in New Orleans and allow you to see all parts of the city. What impressed me the most is the ability to see out to Lake Pontchartrain and the realization this city is actually quite narrow, wedged as it is between the lake and the Mississippi River.

Lafayette Square sits across from Gallier Hall, which served as City Hall for nearly a century. It is the second-oldest public park in New Orleans, behind only Jackson Square. Today Lafayette Square is the site of many free festivals throughout the year, as well as the popular **Wednesday at the Square** (ylcnola.org/ylc-wednesday-at-the-square) concert series. Held each March through mid-May, this free series features well-known local musicians, artisans, and food vendors. Popular with the CBD business crowds, it is also a fun time for tourists and local families. If these events are going on during your stay, be sure to attend.

St. Patrick's Cathedral (oldstpatricks.org; 724 Camp St.; 504-525-4413) was established in 1833 and is significant because it dates back to the early expansion of the city into what is known as the American Sector. After the Louisiana Purchase in 1803, Americans from around the country began moving to New Orleans. When they found it difficult to blend in with the Creole population of the French Quarter, they moved upriver across Canal Street and established their own neighborhoods. Many of the grand hotels and other structures from that period are gone, but St. Patrick's remains.

The **Saenger Theatre** (saengernola.com; 1111 Canal. St.; 504-525-1052) was first opened in 1925. Destroyed by Hurricane Katrina in 2005, it underwent a multiyear renovation before reopening in 2013. This historic theater provides a full schedule of music and plays each year, in addition to many special events.

Caesars Superdome (caesarssuperdome.com; 1500 Sugar Bowl Dr.; 800-756-7074). Opened in 1975, the Superdome is home of the New Orleans Saints, the Sugar Bowl, the Bayou Classic, Essence Fest, and numerous other large concerts and special events throughout the year. The Dome has hosted eight Super Bowls and is the largest domed structure in the world, with a diameter of 680 feet and a roof that covers 13 acres.

Across the street from the Superdome is its baby sister, the **Smoothie King Center** (smoothiekingcenter.com; 1501 Dave Dixon Dr.; 504-587-3663). The center is home to the NBA's New Orleans Pelicans as well as many concerts and special events throughout the year.

The Central Business District is also home to numerous murals and outdoor points of interest. Both the **Riverwalk** and the **Morial Convention Center** structures were part of the 1984 World's Fair. Duck through the Riverwalk and head out to the riverfront for great views of the river and the traffic.

As you stand in the parking lot of the Riverwalk and look towards the French Quarter, you'll find a large mural of a whale, known locally as the **Whale Wall.** Head down Convention Center Boulevard (again, away from the French Quarter) and you'll come upon **Mississippi River Heritage Park.** This small park features a Hurricane Katrina sculpture of a house lodged in a tree.

A couple short blocks away is **Nesbit's Poeyfarre Market.** A good place to duck in for a cold bottle of water and a snack, the real attraction is out front, where you'll find a gondola car, one of the few remnants of that 1984 World's Fair.

Just off Poydras Street, behind the shuttered Little Gem Saloon, is the **Buddy Bolden mural** paying homage to New Orleans's roots as the birthplace of jazz. The mural was created by local artist BMike and

Buddy Bolden mural **MARK BOLOGNA**

is based on the only known photo of the great Buddy Bolden. Bolden is pictured alongside other jazz musicians who played the Little Gem and the nearby Eagle Saloon, both of which were a part of "Black Storyville," a portion of the infamous red-light district of the late 1800s and early 1900s. The Eagle Saloon is also shuttered, but in front is a painted electric box celebrating its past.

A couple of blocks away is the **Holiday Inn.** On the side of it is another mural celebrating jazz music. This one is a clarinet that runs up the height of the building. It is definitely worth seeing. Around the back side of the hotel is a wall painted in a modern art style. Look closely and you'll make out the face of Louis Armstrong, who grew up nearby.

Louis Armstrong mural **MARK BOLOGNA**

Holiday Inn clarinet **MARK BOLOGNA**

THE FAUBOURG MARIGNY

This area of New Orleans is immediately downriver of the French Quarter and is often referred to by locals as "the Marigny" or "the Marigny Triangle." As the triangle implies, it shares Esplanade Avenue with the French Quarter as its upriver border. Downriver, the neighborhood blends into the Bywater at Franklin Avenue. It's back border is St. Claude Avenue, while its smallest border is the Mississippi River. Some locals will argue the triangle stops at Elysian Fields, but neighborhood boundaries are a frequent point of disagreement among locals.

Marigny hibiscus **MARK BOLOGNA**

Faubourg is a French word typically meaning "suburb" and usually used when referring to the suburbs of Paris. The Marigny is named after its former owner, the larger-than-life Bernard de Marigny. When he parceled off the lots in 1806, he created the neighborhood we now recognize as the Marigny. He named one of the streets Craps (now gone), said to be a game he brought to Louisiana from his native country.

The neighborhood is also known for its famous residents of the past. Jazz greats who made this neighborhood their home include Jelly Roll Morton, Danny Barker, Sidney Bechet, and Paul Barbarin, among others.

Today the Marigny is known for its quirky bars, live music along Frenchmen Street, and brightly colored Creole cottages. While Frenchmen Street has become known among locals as the new Bourbon Street for the crowds it draws on some evenings, the neighborhood is generally quiet during the day and well worth exploring, day or night.

EAT

I may have mentioned these previously in the French Quarter section, but **Port of Call** (portofcallnola.com; 838 Esplanade Ave.; 504-523-0120) and **Buffa's Bar & Restaurant** (buffasbar.com; 1001 Esplanade Ave.; 504-949-0038), both on Esplanade Avenue, are worth keeping in mind as you leave the French Quarter and enter the Marigny. Buffa's is a fun spot for both live music and a good casual meal of pub food. It's kid friendly, too.

Buffa's Bar JAMES CULLEN

Port of Call is the place to go for a burger and a strong tiki cocktail in this part of New Orleans. Both are large and delicious. The burgers come with a loaded baked potato and make for a hearty meal. Expect a wait during peak hours. The good news is you can grab a drink at the bar, wait outside, and make new friends.

Dat Dog (datdog.com; 601 Frenchmen St.; 504-309-3362) is a local and very good chain right up Frenchmen Street that serves a variety of hot dogs and sausages paired with a selection of local craft beers.

Loretta's Authentic Pralines (lorettaspralines.com; 2101 N. Rampart St.; 504-944-7068). Closer to St. Claude Avenue, Loretta's serves breakfast and lunch, but the real reason you want to stop in here is for the beignets. Try the praline-stuffed beignets for a real treat!

Budsi's Authentic Thai (budsisthai.com; 1760 N. Rampart St.; 504-381-4636) began its life as a pop-up but now lives in a Creole cottage on the edge of the Marigny. This popular spot serves Thai food with an emphasis on the flavors of the Issan region of that country. The tom yum soup is some of the best I've ever eaten. The drunken noodles or the pad thai are excellent selections for your main course.

The Elysian Bar (theelysianbar.com; 2317 Burgundy St.; 504-356-6769), located within the Hotel Peter and Paul, is a beautiful setting for brunch or dinner, with a small but ample menu including Louisiana seafood as well as chicken and steaks. Prices are a bit on the high side, but this is a great spot for brunch with a friend or a date night.

St. Roch Market (strochmarket.com; 2381 St. Claude Ave.; 504-267-0388) might technically be in the 7th Ward neighborhood, but only because it is on the lake side of St. Claude Avenue. At the time of this writing, the 150-year-old market is home to 11 vendors covering a range of dining options, including but not limited to **CR Coffee Shop, Aritza's Kitchen** for Cuban food, **Laksa** for Burmese, and **The Salted Pearl** for raw oysters.

Baldwin & Co. (baldwinandcobooks.com; 1030 Elysian Fields Ave.; 504-354-1741) is a bookshop and coffee place that opened to a lot of buzz in February 2021. The small selection of books is complemented by excellent coffee and cozy spaces. As a bonus, they also offer a podcast studio that can be reserved.

DRINK

My favorite place for a good cocktail in the Marigny is the aforementioned **Elysian Bar.** The drinks are well made, but the environment is the real draw for me. The bar itself is cozy and welcoming, while the front parlor is the perfect space to meet up with a friend or to get some work done while also enjoying an alcoholic drink (my favorite way to do research for the podcast!).

Brieux Carre Brewing Company's (brieuxcarre.com; 2115 Decatur St.; 504-304-4242) motto is "Stay funky and embrace the weird." A perfect slogan given its location in the Marigny, it is also a good description of their well-crafted beer. Recent examples of their offerings include The Bamburglar, a smoked amber lager; Lil Grey Phantom, a wheat beer; and Nank Dugs, a West Coast IPA.

The aforementioned **Buffa's** is your typical neighborhood bar/restaurant, but it also has a consistently good lineup of live music. The drinks aren't anything special, but its combination of food, music, and drinks is hard to beat.

The Marigny and its neighbor, the Bywater, are known for being eccentric. To underline that point, you'll find a couple of establishments along St. Claude Avenue worth checking out.

I'm not sure whether to put the **Allways Lounge** (theallwayslounge.net; 2240 St. Claude Ave.; 504-321-5606) under places to drink or things to see and do. You might find a peep show, a cabaret, cat acrobats, or a comedian on any given night. Bonus if local burlesque dancer Trixie Minx is performing. No matter what, you'll have a fun and memorable time.

Cafe Istanbul (cafeistanbulnola.com; 2327 St. Claude Ave.; 504-975-0286) continues the trend of bars that offer more than a place to imbibe. On any given night the lineup may include dance, live music, theater, comedy, a poetry reading, or some combination of these.

Frenchmen Street is a more on-the-beaten-path place to go for live music in the Marigny, though still worth your time one evening. You'll find several options offering all manner of drinks, though I tend to stick with craft beer in most of these. Their focus is the music, of course, but it is nice to have drinks available while you listen.

In a two-block stretch you'll encounter **The Maison, Cafe Negril, d.b.a., The Spotted Cat, Blue Nile,** and **Three Muses.** All are fun places with live music. Your best bet is to walk this stretch first, then enter the club that draws you in with the music coming through the front door.

If you are hungry, **Three Muses** (3musesnola.com; 536 Frenchmen St.; 504-252-4801) offers the best selection of small plates. You'll find a bowl of chicken and andouille gumbo and a Korean po-boy among the 10 or so plates on the menu.

THE BYWATER

The next neighborhood downriver from the Marigny is the Bywater. The funkiness of the Marigny continues with colorful houses, hole-in-the-wall bars, good food, and plenty of street art. This is an area considered trendy in New Orleans but is still largely undiscovered by visitors. The shape of this neighborhood is sort of a backwards J, but for our purposes it includes, not surprisingly, the area nearest the Mississippi River and Poland Avenue along the Industrial Canal.

EAT

Satsuma Cafe (satsumacafe.com; 3218 Dauphine St.; 504-304-5692) is self-described as a hipster-friendly coffee bar. I think that undersells it. In addition to great coffee, they make in-house juices and serve breakfast and light lunch options, all with a focus on locally sourced organic ingredients. If you are looking for a healthy breakfast option or a lunch spot after walking from the French Quarter, the Satsuma Cafe is a solid choice.

Alma Cafe (eatalmanola.com; 800 Louisa St.; 504-381-5877) is a half block from Satsuma. This Honduran restaurant is a terrific spot for breakfast or lunch. I'm partial to the breakfast: plantains and pancakes, with a café con leche. Alma is a good choice for catching up with a friend or doing business. It's cheery and bright, and there are options on the menu for exploring Honduran cuisine or choosing the tried and true.

Pizza Delicious (pizzadelicious.com; 617 Piety St.; 504-676-8482) started as a weird pop-up where you called a cell phone to place your order and were given an address for pickup that was down an alley. Flash-forward 10-plus years, and the two New York–born friends that started the place serve some of the best pizza in town. Huge slices of New York–style pizza are complemented by pastas and salads.

Bratz Y'all (bratzyall.com; 617 Piety St.; 504-301-3222). Sharing an address with Pizza Delicious, this German beer garden serves the usual German fare of bratwurst, schnitzel, and pretzels, as well as an award-winning "Drunk Pig" po-boy. The Drunk Pig is my favorite, but there is nothing on the menu I don't enjoy. If you are hungry, get the schnitzel—it is a ridiculously large portion.

Plenty of outdoor seating, a regular offering of live music, and a large selection of German beer make this a fun place to while away an

Bratz Y'all **MARK BOLOGNA**

afternoon. I've written a good portion of the book you're reading sitting at a Bratz Y'all picnic bench while nibbling a warm pretzel. There may or may not have been beer involved!

Note: If you are in New Orleans during Carnival, try their pretzel king cake. It is a pretzel sliced open and filled with Bavarian cream. It is consistently one of the favorite nontraditional king cakes at my house.

Euclid Records (euclidrecordsneworleans.com; 3301 Chartres St.; 504-947-4348). While obviously not a place to eat, I mention it here because if you've eaten next door at Bratz Y'all and have any interest in new or used vinyl, you'll want to stop in. They sometimes have live music, too.

Bywater American Bistro (babs-nola.com; 2900 Chartres St.; 504-605-3827) is an upscale neighborhood restaurant. This is the sister restaurant to Chef Nina Compton's Compère Lapin, located in the Old No. 77 Hotel in the Central Business District. The menu is as eclectic as the neighborhood. Recent offerings included curried rabbit, jerk chicken, pork belly, and fried snapper. A fun place for date night.

Elizabeth's (elizabethsrestaurantnola.com; 601 Gallier St.; 504-944-9272) is a popular place for breakfast, brunch, and lunch, with good reason. The menu includes standard breakfast fare as well as a nod to New Orleans with items like the Lula Mae Breakfast Po-Boy. Gumbo, burgers, and po-boys make up the lunch menu, and there is a small bar if you want to imbibe while you eat.

INSIDER TIP: Go early to Elizabeth's or expect to wait.

Bywater Bakery (bywaterbakery.com; 3624 Dauphine St.; 504-336-3336) is best known for its king cakes, but is a solid choice for breakfast, including its house-made bagels.

The Joint (alwayssmokin.com; 701 Mazant St.; 504-949-3232). New Orleans is not known for BBQ, but there are a few notable exceptions and the Joint is one of them. Expect the usual wide assortment of smoked meats, and pair them with a cocktail or daiquiri from the bar.

Capulet (capuletbywater.com; 3014 Dauphine St.; 504-507-0691) is a nice spot for breakfast or lunch, with several vegan and vegetarian options and great cocktails. Thursday evenings include live music and a jam session.

Sneaky Pickle (yousneakypickle.com; 4017 St. Claude Ave.; 504-218-5651) is a New Orleans favorite for vegetarians. The menu changes frequently and focuses on fresh local ingredients. The place doesn't look like much, but if you are vegetarian, this is where you want to go for lunch while exploring the Bywater and the Marigny.

DRINK

Bacchanal Wine (bacchanalwine.com; 600 Poland Ave.; 504-948-9111) is in the downriver corner of the Bywater, near the point at which the Industrial Canal meets the Mississippi River. The largely Mediterranean menu is excellent, but not the reason you come here. You visit Bacchanal to drink one of the hundreds of wine selections with friends while enjoying the open-air patio and the daily stream of live music. This is one of the best spots in New Orleans to while away an afternoon with friends or fellow travelers.

Parleaux Beer Lab (parleauxbeerlab.com; 634 Lesseps St.; 504-702-8433). If craft beer is your jam, head around the corner to this microbrewery that features a small but ample taproom, as well as outdoor space. The locally made beers are wide ranging and well crafted. Recent selections include a Czech-style pilsner, a Vienna lager, a juicy double IPA made with local satsumas, and a Scottish brown ale. Typically, you can expect about eight beers on the menu.

New Orleans has experienced a big growth in the craft beer scene over the last several years. Parleaux is among the best and is a must-stop for the beer lover.

Bar Redux (barredux.tumblr.com; 801 Poland Ave.; 504-592-7083) is yet another funky place that fits the neighborhood vibe. Notice the website is a Tumblr account! It's a chill place to enjoy live music on their patio. The drink menu is pretty simple, but this dive is a perfectly fine, off-the-beaten-path spot to enjoy the music and the sounds of the nearby Mississippi River traffic.

B.J.'s Lounge (4301 Burgundy St.; 504-945-9256). If dive bars with live music and a good jukebox are your thing, check out B.J.'s Lounge. Friendly patrons and fun bartenders make this a classic neighborhood place to hang out.

Bud Rip's (900 Piety St.; 504-945-5762) and **Markey's Bar** (markeysbar.com; 640 Louisa St.; 504-943-0785) are two others that fit this vibe. Markey's has good pub food, while Bud Rip's has taco Tuesdays, bingo on Wednesdays, and a pool table.

Vaughan's Lounge (4229 Dauphine St.; 504-947-5562) is well-known among locals for live music on Thursdays and cheap drinks. Fans of the HBO series *Treme* might recognize Vaughan's for its appearance in the very first episode, when Elvis Costello drops in to listen to Kermit Ruffins and his BBQ Swingers perform. Over the years many famous musicians have dropped by, including Lenny Kravitz, members of the Rolling Stones, and New Orleans's own Harry Connick Jr.

The Country Club (thecountryclubneworleans.com; 634 Louisa St.; 504-945-0742). I'm not sure where to put the Country Club, so I'll drop it here. It's a restaurant. It's a bar. It's a pool. Once upon a time the pool was clothing optional, but (thankfully!?) those days are long gone. Today, it's a popular spot for brunch, as well as for those who just want to grab a drink in a lovely environment. The pool is very popular, so if a drink and a dip sound like fun, give it a go.

Bywater Brew Pub (bywaterbrewpub.com; 3000 Royal St.; 504-766-8118) serves beer brewed in-house as well as a selection of craft beers from other local breweries. Billed as a gastropub, the menu is a

Vaughan's **JAMES CULLEN**

combination of Louisiana meets Vietnamese—a product of Chef Anh Luu's ancestry as a New Orleans native born to Vietnamese refugees.

SEE & DO

The Bywater is full of street art and murals. If you enjoy photography, this is a neighborhood you'll want to explore.

At the corner of Royal and Homer Plessy Way is **Plessy Park,** a small park with a large mural named *These Are Times* and a historical marker. There are no known pictures of Homer Plessy, so the mural depicts his legacy and those who came after him in the fight for civil rights. Nearby is a large image painted on a building of what Homer Plessy might have looked like.

BMike mural **MARK BOLOGNA**

HOMER PLESSY

On June 7, 1892, Homer Plessy was removed from a railroad car at the intersection of Royal and Press Streets (now Homer Plessy Way) and arrested. The arrest was fully expected and was a deliberate act in order to challenge segregation laws in the South. While the Supreme Court ultimately ruled against Plessy in 1896, it was an important first step in the fight to use the 14th Amendment's "equal protection" clause as a means of gaining equal rights for African Americans in the United States.

Homer Plessy mural **MARK BOLOGNA**

Studio Be (bmike.com; 2941 Royal St.; 504-252-0463) is in the same block as Plessy Park. Studio Be is the creation of artist Brandan "BMike" Odums and features large-scale artwork created by BMike and others. One exhibit in the 35,000-square-foot space is *Radical Freedom Dream*, the product of a series of workshops for kids.

Crescent Park cyclist **JAMES CULLEN**

Crescent Park runs along the Mississippi River and provides a unique view looking back at downtown New Orleans. Walkers, runners, and cyclists make frequent use of this linear park, and photographers like to take pictures of the **Rusty Rainbow Bridge,** which goes over a set of railroad tracks.

Music Box Village (musicboxvillage.com; 4557 N. Rampart St.) is a unique art installation composed of interactive "music houses" created by local artists. The village is the product of New Orleans Airlift, a non-profit dedicated to helping artists primarily through education and the creation of public art displays.

Music Box Village is off the beaten path but is well worth the time and effort to get there. New Orleans Airlift has occasionally sponsored temporary installations of the Music Box Village at various places across the city. At Jazz Fest, they install a three-story musical tower in the children's area—I enjoy it as much as my kids!

Just to the right of the village, there are train tracks. Near those tracks is a section of street art depicting Harriet Tubman. Sitting as it does right against the tracks, the symbolism is quite powerful. It is one of my favorite pieces of street art in New Orleans.

Harriet Tubman mural **MARK BOLOGNA**

From here, walk along the levee out to the intersection of the Industrial Canal. This spot, sometimes called "the End of the World" by locals, is close to Bacchanal and has a great view of river traffic. You'll see people walking dogs, photographing the nearby street art, and enjoying the breeze.

TREMÉ

The Tremé is the oldest African-American neighborhood in the United States and one of the oldest sections of New Orleans. It sits directly behind the French Quarter and is sometimes called "back of town" or "backatown" by locals. The Tremé is home to a rich African-American and Creole culture. It also includes Congo Square, a reminder of the terrible hardships endured by slaves in America.

The Tremé has always been well-known locally as fertile ground for New Orleans brass bands, Creole food, and Mardi Gras Indians. In 2010 the HBO series *Treme* introduced this vibrant neighborhood and its traditions to a wide audience.

As with most neighborhoods in New Orleans, the boundaries are somewhat malleable. For our purposes, the river side of the Tremé is Rampart Street. The downriver boundary is Esplanade, while upriver it is Canal Street. The back of the Tremé is N. Broad Street.

EAT & DRINK

The word *Creole* is often applied to people, culture, and food in New Orleans. When it comes to food, it is loosely defined as city or urban food, compared to Cajun, which tends to be food that comes from the country, and more specifically the southwestern part of Louisiana. In the Tremé that Creole culture and its culinary traditions are found in its neighborhood restaurants.

Dooky Chase's (dookychaserestaurants.com; 2301 Orleans Ave.; 504-821-0600) is the most famous and culturally significant restaurant in the Tremé. Chef Leah Chase presided over the restaurant for seven decades until her death in 2019. During that time, Chef Leah welcomed locals, civil rights activists, politicians, and even US presidents to dinner. The restaurant is filled with artwork created by African-American artists. Dooky Chase's is widely known by locals as a wonderful place to enjoy red beans and rice, fried chicken, and peach cobbler.

Lunch at Dooky Chase's on Holy Thursday is one of the most coveted reservations in New Orleans. On that day (and only that day) the menu includes Chef Leah's Gumbo Z'Herbes, a vegetarian version of gumbo said to be made with nine different herbs. The vegetarian version is a nod to New Orleans's Catholic roots on one of the most significant days in the Church. Chef Leah's daughter Stella Chase has continued the tradition of producing nearly 100 gallons of the highly sought-after dish.

I only got to attend Holy Thursday lunch at Dooky Chase's a single time, but it was unforgettable. In addition to the food and the guests that filled the dining room, I will always remember Chef Leah coming out to welcome the crowd with a few words, then stopping by each table to say hello. She rarely forgot a face and could recall something about nearly everyone she had met before.

Willie Mae's Scotch House (williemaesnola.com; 2401 St. Ann St.; 504-822-9503) is around the corner from Dooky Chase's. Willie Mae's is known for its crispy fried chicken, which the Travel Channel named "America's best fried chicken" in 2007. Like Chef Leah Chase, Willie Mae Seaton received a James Beard Award for her efforts and her restaurant's significance in the culinary world. The fried chicken is a must-have, but the menu is full of soul food dishes like fried okra, butter beans, candied yams, and more.

Lil' Dizzie's Cafe (lildizzyscafe.net; 1500 Esplanade Ave.; 504-766-8687) is the epitome of a New Orleans neighborhood place. The menu includes fried chicken, gumbo, po-boys, seafood plates, and daily specials like red beans, smothered okra, and pork chops. Longtime owner Eddie Baquet stepped away from the restaurant in 2021, but his son has taken over with a commitment to continue the family tradition.

Gabrielle Restaurant (gabriellerestaurant.com; 2441 Orleans Ave.; 504-603-2344) does not fit the mold of the typical Tremé restaurant, but is perfect for a nice dinner not far from the French Quarter. Chefs Mary and Greg Sonnier opened Gabrielle in 1992 on Esplanade Avenue not far from City Park. The restaurant, named after their daughter, was shuttered by Hurricane Katrina and remained closed until 2017, when it reopened at its present location. Best known for its gumbo and roasted duck, I'm partial to the BBQ shrimp pie followed by the double-cut pork chop. Reservations required.

Sweet Soulfood (sweetvegansoulfood.com; 1025 N. Broad St.; 504-821-2669) is what happens when you combine a classic New Orleans–style neighborhood eatery with a vegan menu. Food is served from a steam table as diners point to their selections. From red beans and rice to stuffed bell peppers, there is something on the menu you'll enjoy, even if you are not vegan.

Vaucresson's Sausage Company (vaucressonsausage.com; 1800 St. Bernard Ave.; 855-727-3653). Technically in the 7th Ward, this casual lunch stop is the place for sausage. Try their hot sausage or jerked chicken sausage po-boys.

Note: Vance Vaucresson is a second-generation sausage maker, and carries on his father's tradition of serving his po-boys at the annual Jazz and Heritage Festival. Vaucresson's is the only original vendor at the festival, a testament to their food and commitment.

Kermit's Tremé Mother-in-Law Lounge (kermitslounge.com; 1500 N. Claiborne Ave.; 504-975-3955) is technically a lounge and music venue, but it fits here better than any other section in this chapter. No matter, this is a fun spot for live music and cheap drinks, especially when Kermit Ruffins is there to light up the room with his trumpet, his voice, and his personality.

There is also a story behind the lounge. As the name implies, it comes from the late Ernie K-Doe's famous hit single "Mother in Law." K-Doe referred to himself as the Emperor of the Universe and owned this bar with his wife, Antoinette. The Emperor died in 2001 and Antoinette followed in 2009. Kermit later purchased the lounge and continued the tradition of a larger-than-life music personality operating the Mother-in-Law.

SEE & DO

Directly behind the French Quarter on Rampart Street, you enter **Louis Armstrong Park** through a lighted archway bearing the jazz trumpeter's name. The park is 31 acres and includes Congo Square and the Mahalia Jackson Theater for the Performing Arts. Concerts, festivals, and other events are regularly held in the park that celebrates the birth of jazz.

Armstrong Park band statue **JAMES CULLEN**

Armstrong Park arch dog walker **JAMES CULLEN**

Congo Square was a place where slaves and free persons of color could gather throughout the 19th century. There they held markets and celebrated their African culture through dance and drumming. It is the music and drumming of Congo Square that influenced early musicians in New Orleans and led to the creation of jazz.

Also within the confines of Louis Armstrong Park, you'll find a statue honoring **Chief Allison "Tootie" Montana** (1922–2005). Known as the Big Chief for over 50 years, he helped lead and preserve the Mardi Gras Indian culture of New Orleans. The Big Chief played a major role in shifting the Mardi Gras Indian traditions away from violence and replaced them with a celebration of the artistry and the rituals we see today. Prior to Chief Montana, Mardi Gras Indian suits were plain and simple. He began adding brightly colored ostrich feathers and colorful beads formed into elaborate shapes.

The **Backstreet Cultural Museum** (backstreetmuseum.org; 1116 Henriette Delille St.; 504-606-4809) is a small museum housed inside a building that once was a mortuary. It was created by Sylvester Francis to celebrate African-American culture in New Orleans. The museum houses a large collection of Mardi Gras Indian suits, as well as information about second lines, social aid and pleasure clubs, the Baby Dolls, and the Northside Skull and Bones Gang.

I could easily devote several pages of this book to every one of these important New Orleans traditions, but you'll have a much better appreciation by visiting this cash-only museum. Highly recommended.

St. Augustine Catholic Church (staugchurch.org; 1210 Governor Nicholls St.; 504-525-5934). In the same block as the Backstreet Cultural Museum, St. Augustine was founded in 1841 and is the oldest African-American Catholic parish in the country. The pews are original to the church itself, which was dedicated in October 1842. It was a common practice to charge a fee for church pews at that time, and free men of color paid extra so that enslaved people could attend.

Today parishioners and visitors alike attend the very popular Gospel Jazz Mass on Sundays. In a garden next to the church is the **Tomb of the Unknown Slave.** The monument is a cross made of iron chains. The location is also significant since the land was the site of Tremé Plantation House.

Lafitte Greenway street art MARK BOLOGNA

The **Lafitte Greenway** (lafittegreenway.org) is a 2.6-mile linear park that links the Tremé with Bayou St.

John in the Midcity neighborhood near several bars, restaurants, and a bakery. It includes a walking and bicycle trail, park space, playgrounds, and outdoor works of art. It was opened in 2015 and has become a popular place for New Orleanians to enjoy the outdoors.

St. Louis Cemetery #1 and #2 (nolacatholiccemeteries.org/our cemeteries; #1 is at 425 Basin St., #2 is at 300 N. Claiborne Ave.). I've grouped these together because they are just a few blocks apart. St. Louis #1 was established in 1798 and is the oldest cemetery still existing in New Orleans. You can only visit with a tour guide. (I suggest my podcast sponsor Two Chicks Walking Tours, twochickswalkingtours .com, for this tour and others.)

The way we bury people aboveground in New Orleans is unique and reflects part of our culture and our relationship with the land and the Mississippi River. The crypts themselves are often beautiful, if not a bit haunting.

If you visit St. Louis #1, you'll see the rumored grave of Marie Laveau, the famous voodoo queen. Laveau is believed to have shared her family's tomb with as many as 30 other people who did not have a place or the resources to bury their own. You'll also see a pyramid-shaped tomb that looks completely out of place. The plot was purchased some years ago by actor Nicholas Cage. I think it's ridiculous that it is there, but it is, so you might as well check it out for yourself.

St. Louis #2 is only a few blocks away, but is far less visited. While St. Louis #1 is just outside the French Quarter, #2 feels quite isolated. I would be aware of your surroundings if you do visit, and would advise doing so only if you have a vehicle or a bike. It is not that it is unsafe—I just don't like to send people unfamiliar with the area to a place where you may be the only person around. While it doesn't get the attention of #1, its tombs are quite old and beautiful in their own way.

For the best book about the cemeteries, I recommend Sally Asher's excellent *Stories from the St. Louis Cemeteries of New Orleans*. Sally was a guest on the *Beyond Bourbon Street* podcast (episode 57) as well. The thing that makes Sally's book such a fascinating read is she tells the stories of the people buried in the three St. Louis cemeteries.

Teaser alert: When you get to the chapter of this book about the Midcity neighborhood, you'll read about St. Louis #3. Of the three, it is my favorite.

The **New Orleans African American Museum** (noaam.org; 1417-18 Governor Nichols St.; 504-218-8254) was created to preserve the art, culture, and history of African Americans in New Orleans. The land that is now home to the museum was originally the Morand Plantation and later owned by Claude Tremé, which is how we got the name of the neighborhood. This small museum is a hidden gem and worth your

Trumpet Black mural **JAMES CULLEN**

time. They also host many special events throughout the year, so be sure to check their website in advance of your visit to New Orleans.

On Esplanade Avenue among the shade of the live oak trees, you'll find three places worth visiting. The first you'll come to if walking from the French Quarter is the **Gayarré Place** monument called **Peace, the Genius of History.** The monument is located at the intersection of Esplanade and Bayou Road. There are two things that make this monument and park noteworthy.

The first is that the monument was originally built for and displayed at the 1884 New Orleans World's Industrial and Cotton Exposition, commonly called the World's Fair. This World's Fair was the first of two that would be held in New Orleans (the other in 1984 in the Central Business District and Warehouse District) and was based in what is now Audubon Park.

The second noteworthy thing is the placement and shape of the small park itself. Whenever you see a small triangular park in New Orleans, it typically signifies the intersection of property lines from old plantations. As those plantations were parceled and sold off, the surveyors would be left with an odd-shaped wedge of land, particularly if the adjoining properties were not surveyed at the same time. As a result, most of these wedges of land became pocket parks, as is the case here.

Degas House (degashouse.com; 2306 Esplanade Ave.; 504-821-5009), across the street from the park, serves today as both a bed-and-breakfast and a very small museum. The Degas House is so named because the artist came to New Orleans in 1872 to visit his uncle and his brothers. His mother, Célestine Musson, was born in the city, so Degas had been fascinated by it since his youth. I would not make a special trip to visit, but if you are in the area, it is a quick stop and worth a few minutes of your time.

Le Musée de f.p.c. (lemuseedefpc.com; 2336 Esplanade Ave.; 504-323-5074), which stands for "free people of color," is on the same block as the Degas House. While New Orleans was the center of slavery, there were many free people of color in the city, and many of them settled in the Tremé. This museum is dedicated to telling their stories and contributions to New Orleans. Call ahead to set up a visit.

ALGIERS & THE WEST BANK

Algiers is the second-oldest neighborhood in New Orleans and the only part of the city located on the west bank of the Mississippi River.

Algiers Point is the part of the neighborhood you'll want to experience as a visitor. The easiest and best way to get there is to take the **Canal Street Passenger Ferry** from the dock just beyond the Audubon Aquarium. You'll disembark right on the levee, which offers a great perspective looking back at the French Quarter as well as the river traffic making the turn that gives New Orleans its nickname Crescent City.

The ferry ride itself is inexpensive and my favorite way to experience the Mississippi River. Cool breezes and an eye-level view of the river traffic provide a unique perspective you won't want to miss. Even if you only ride across, walk on the levee for a few minutes, and ride back across, it is worth your time.

Algiers looking to the French Quarter JAMES CULLEN

EAT & DRINK

Congregation Coffee Roasters (congregationcoffee.com; 240 Pelican Ave.; 504-265-0194). If you cross the river early in the day and need a cup of coffee, stop in. It's just a few blocks from the ferry terminal.

Crown & Anchor English Pub (crownandanchor.pub; 200 Pelican Ave.; 504-227-1007). Try this pub if you need something a little stronger. You enter the traditional pub through a blue police box. English and local brews make up the beer menu, in addition to the very good Scotch and whiskey offerings.

Barracuda (eatbarracuda.com; 446 Pelican St.; 504-766-7268) offers street tacos and margaritas with outdoor seating. Be sure to try their chips and queso with pomegranate seeds.

Old Point Bar (oldpointbarnola.com; 545 Patterson St.; 504-364-0950) offers live music and bar food in a lively environment typically filled with locals who'll look up from their drinks when you enter. Don't let them scare you away. Grab a seat at the bar and soak up the vibe.

FURTHER AFIELD ON THE WEST BANK

While most visitors won't venture beyond Algiers Point, there are several other restaurants worth your attention on the West Bank.

Mosca's (moscasrestaurant.com; 4137 US Highway 90 West; 504-436-8950) is known for their huge family-style portions of New Orleans Italian dishes including Oysters Mosca, chicken cacciatore, and Chicken a la Grande—sautéed with rosemary and Italian seasonings, cloves of garlic, and white wine. If you have a group, Mosca's is well worth the 20- to 30-minute drive from the French Quarter. Casual, but reservations recommended.

Cafe 615 (cafe615.com; 615 Kepler St.; 504-365-1225). If you've been to Joey K's on Magazine Street, think of this as the West Bank version, though they are not affiliated. Big portions, including an excellent muffaletta. The fried boneless pork cops are delicious at this casual neighborhood spot, just a few minutes over the Mississippi River Bridge and not far from Algiers Point.

Hi Do Bakery (439 Terry Pkwy.; 504-366-6555). This bakery makes one of my favorite king cakes when in season. Also available at the King Cake Hub in New Orleans during Carnival.

Chubbie's Fried Chicken (4850 General Meyer Ave.; 504-392-2377). This nondescript restaurant in a slightly rundown area has maybe my favorite fried chicken in the city. Large pieces, crispy and juicy, served with a biscuit and a side—get the dirty rice.

SEE & DO

The **levee in Algiers Point** is the stuff photographers dream of. Great views of both the French Quarter and the heavy river traffic make it one of my favorite spots for capturing images of the original footprint of New Orleans. The levee is also a nice place to get some exercise, and the river offers a breeze even on the hottest summer days.

Close to Old Point Bar is a walkway that leads to the levee. As you climb the steps, there is a mural of a brass band leading the way. It is an ode to the many jazz musicians who called Algiers Point home and is another great spot to capture a photo.

Closer to the ferry terminal the levee is home to the **Jazz Walk of Fame,** where you can walk from lamppost to lamppost and learn about famous New Orleans jazz musicians at each stop.

The **Algiers Historical Society** created several self-guided walking tours (algiershistoricalsociety.org/walking-tours.html) that can be downloaded to your phone. This is the best way to wander the Point while learning about the music, the architecture, and the history. While following the tours, you'll also pass by many examples of the Victorian-style architecture common in this neighborhood.

For more information about Algiers Point, listen to episode 30 of my *Beyond Bourbon Street* podcast.

GARDEN DISTRICT & LOWER GARDEN DISTRICT

Two things New Orleanians like to disagree about are neighborhood boundaries and how to pronounce street names. Both of these are going to come up in the next few chapters.

The Garden District is typically referred to in two parts. The section closest to Downtown is called the Lower Garden District. My local friends who read this will want to argue the next point, but for our purposes the boundaries of the Lower Garden District are Calliope on the downriver (downtown) side, Jackson Avenue (uptown), St. Charles Avenue on the lake side, and Tchoupitoulas Street along the Mississippi River.

House and plants **MARK BOLOGNA**

In case you've forgotten or skipped the earlier section on geography, we don't use compass directions in New Orleans. Everything is oriented based on its relationship to the river (upriver or downriver, sometimes uptown or downtown) and to Lake Pontchartrain.

The Garden District is bounded by Jackson, Magazine, St. Charles, and Toledano. For reasons unknown to me, this area is not called the Upper Garden District, but simply the Garden District.

With that out of the way, the Lower Garden District and the Irish Channel, the Garden District, and Uptown make up a contiguous part of the city that largely blend into each other as they meander up the Mississippi River towards Jefferson Parish. These areas are easily and best explored on foot. If you are staying in the French Quarter or Central Business District, you are a short streetcar ride away.

To limit the amount of rancor from locals and to make this area easier for you to explore, I am grouping some neighborhoods together. From a practical point of view, it will make no difference.

As we begin exploring the area from the Lower Garden District all the way to Audubon Park, there are four main streets that run parallel to the river and provide a good organizing structure for us. They are St. Charles Avenue, Prytania Street, Magazine Street, and Tchoupitoulas Street. Each of them makes periodic gentle turns as they head upriver to mirror the turns in the Mississippi.

EAT

The first two stops I recommend for dining on St. Charles also happen to be good spots to enjoy an adult beverage.

Lula Restaurant Distillery (lulanola.com; 1532 St. Charles Ave.; 504-267-7624) is a micro distillery that makes rum, vodka, and gin. My favorite menu items include crawfish queso, boudin egg rolls (boudin is a sausage made with rice and pork), and shrimp and grits, though there is more-standard fare if you would prefer. Large umbrellas shield you from the sun if the weather is nice and you would like to sit outside.

The Avenue Pub (theavenuepub.com; 1732 St. Charles Ave.; 504-586-9243). Find it two blocks up St. Charles. Consistently rated the best beer bar in the city and one of the best in the country, it is also one of my favorite places to hang out and/or to work on the podcast. A good portion of this book was written on the back patio.

The draft beer menu changes frequently. It is extensive, and includes a wide range of beers made in Louisiana and elsewhere. Helpfully, the paper menus offer a detailed description of each beer. The bartenders are friendly and knowledgeable. Tell them what you like, and they'll match a beer to your taste.

While their reputation for beer is well deserved, the food is excellent. I am a fan of their hummus, grilled chicken, and burgers. The menu changes from time to time, and the food is always better than people expect from a bar. There is indoor seating, but you'll want to sit upstairs on the balcony when the weather is nice. Up there you'll enjoy a breeze and get to watch the streetcars rumble by.

If you need to get some work done, head to the back patio with your laptop and a drink. Say hi if you see me working at the long wooden table!

Mr. John's Steakhouse (mrjohnssteakhouse.com; 211 St. Charles Ave.; 504-679-7697) is the place for steak on St. Charles Avenue. The bustling if sometimes noisy dining room is relaxed compared to most places serving fine steaks. Steaks here are served in the traditional New Orleans style, sizzling in hot butter (this follows in the footsteps of Ruth's Chris Steakhouse, which was founded in New Orleans). Turtle soup or French onion is a good first choice.

Gracious Bakery (graciousbakery.com; 2854 St. Charles Ave.; 504-301-9949). Try this bakery for a light breakfast with excellent coffee. During Carnival they make a variety of king cakes, all of them delicious.

Now we'll head toward Prytania Street and begin our journey from Calliope towards Uptown again.

Commander's Palace (commanderspalace.com; 1403 Washington Ave.; 504-899-8221) is a block off Prytania Street. One of the most well-known and best restaurants in the city continues to earn its reputation. In 2020 Chef Meg Bickford took over the kitchen and became the first female chef to do so. Her predecessors include Emeril Lagasse, Paul Prudhomme, Jamie Shannon, and Tory McPhail.

Like those before her, Chef Bickford has added her twist to the menu in addition to the classics regulars expect. Turtle soup, gumbo, and the shrimp and tasso Henican are sure bets, but the menu also includes a take on the tamale, quail, and Louisiana white shrimp curry. If you like turtle soup, this is the place to get it. Any of the local fish featured as a special will be excellent. I also like the veal chop. The Chef's Playground is a great way to go if you are a bit adventurous—they'll shape the menu based on your preferences.

Commander's is a strong choice for an upscale dinner, but the weekend jazz brunch and lunch are my favorite times to go. Reservations required.

INSIDER TIP: Sit downstairs if you want to be in the middle of everything. Ask for a table in the Garden Room if you want a little less noise. Commander's has 25-cent martinis at lunchtime on Thursdays and Fridays!

Along Magazine Street you'll find lots of great options ranging from super casual to upscale.

Surrey's Cafe and Juice Bar (surreysnola.com; 1418 Magazine St.; 504-524-3828) is a fun and funky spot for breakfast or lunch. The menu includes fresh-squeezed organic juices and items that range from the traditional breakfast to bananas Foster French toast or a crabmeat omelette.

Mojo Coffee House (mojocoffeehouse.com; 1500 Magazine St.) is a good spot for reading, working, or just taking a break.

Gris Gris (grisgrisnola.com; 1800 Magazine St.; 504-272-0241). At Felicity Street, Magazine takes a dogleg turn to the right as it follows the bend in the Mississippi River. Right after this turn is Gris Gris, a polished version of a neighborhood restaurant. Somehow, it manages to feel like the equivalent of business casual dress.

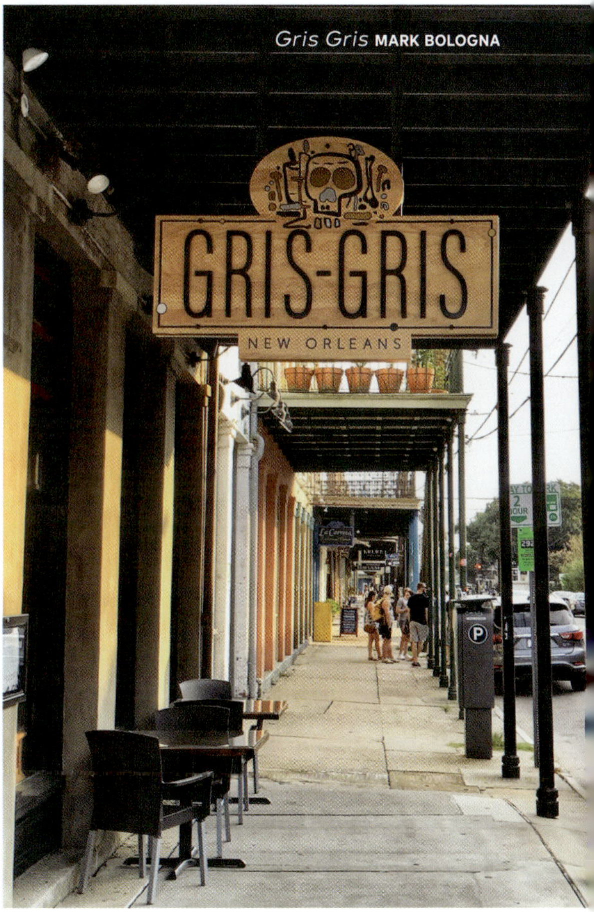

Gris Gris **MARK BOLOGNA**

Downstairs diners eat at the chef's table, where you can watch the kitchen prepare your meals. I prefer the more casual upstairs, which includes a bar, several tables, and a wraparound balcony that is a great spot when the weather is nice.

The menu includes local dishes you'd expect like chicken and andouille gumbo, but it expands to include an oyster BLT, chicken gizzard grillades, sugarcane seared duck, and rabbit fricassee. The gumbo is dark and smoky, and one of my top three in all New Orleans (the others being Brigtsen's and Mr. B's Bistro).

Hivolt (hivoltcoffeepickup.com; 1829 Sophie Wright Place; 504-324-8818) is just down the street from Gris Gris and is my favorite coffee shop in this part of New Orleans.

When you cross Jackson Avenue, you'll come to Stein's Deli and District Donuts, located next to each other.

Stein's Deli (steinsdeli.com; 2207 Magazine St.; 504-527-0771) is a small and very popular place for lunch. It gets crowded during peak hours, so one option is to call your order in ahead of time or get it to go. My favorite sandwich is the Robért with prosciutto, house-made mozzarella, and balsamic vinegar on ciabatta. This is probably my wife's favorite non–New Orleans food place in the city.

INSIDER TIP: Stein's also has a large assortment of beer sold only to go. Don't just look in the coolers: head to the back of the store, go through the back door, cross the alley, and proceed through the next door. You'll be rewarded with another room full of beer, often at discounted prices.

District Donuts (districtdonuts.com; 2209 Magazine St.; 504-570-6945) is your place for "fancy" doughnuts and coffee. The doughnut menu changes often, but my go-to is the buttermilk drop. I could eat my weight in these dipped in coffee, though one is probably where I should stop.

I like this place for business meetings, a quick morning break, or to catch up on email and work on the podcast. The booths are large, and there is a small courtyard out back. District Donuts is popular with my twins, who are not the easiest to please.

Joey Ks (joeyksrestaurant.com; 3001 Magazine St.; 504-891-0997) is a classic New Orleans neighborhood restaurant and the best example in this part of the city. Red beans and rice, a large selection of po-boys, and daily specials are exactly what New Orleanians expect in a place like this. Joey Ks does not disappoint. Everything I've ever eaten here (and that's most of the menu) has been good. The portions are large, which is good if you want to order a few dishes for the table to share.

If you are dining alone, I like the bar to your left when you walk in. It is set back just a bit, which seems to temper the noise.

Empanola (empanolaempanadas.com; 3109 Magazine St.; 504-582-9378) features Latin-inspired, Louisiana-influenced, store-made empanadas in many different flavors including vegetarian options. My favorites include the crawfish étouffée and the gumbo empanadas. Excellent choice for lunch while wandering Magazine Street.

Visiting during Carnival? If so, you'll want to stop in at **Haydel's Bake Shop** (haydelsbakery.com; 3117 Magazine St.; 504-267-3165) and try the king cake.

Dat Dog (datdog.com; 3336 Magazine St.; 504-324-2226). I wrote about Dat Dog in the chapter about the Marigny, but here we come across another location of the local chain. This one features a large outdoor seating space and is a good choice with kids, though I frequently stop in without mine when I want a dog and a beer. Don't tell them!

Coquette (coquettenola.com; 2800 Magazine St.; 504-265-0421) is one of a collection of restaurants along Magazine Street I would put in a category I might describe as casually elegant, gourmet, sophisticated, and intimate. All are perfect for a special occasion.

Coquette meets the above description but feels a little more like a neighborhood gathering spot than some of the others. The bar is the kind of place you might find people meeting after work or for one last drink after a date night. The menu (again, like the others in this category) is what I might describe as adventurous. All of the dishes are centered on fresh ingredients and change constantly. You might find a beef brisket sausage, a fish like cobia, or a chicken roulade. The portions tend to be on the smaller side but are artfully presented.

If you or your partner would describe you as a picky eater, this isn't the place for you. However, if you enjoy food as an exploration of tastes, you'll love Coquette. Reservations required.

The others I would put in this group for fine dining on Magazine Street include **Lilette**, **Bouligny Tavern**, and **La Petite Grocery.** I'll cover each of them in their respective neighborhoods.

DRINK

Barrel Proof (barrelproofnola.com; 1201 Magazine St.). The previously mentioned Avenue Pub is my go-to destination in the Lower Garden District for drinks, but there are many others I enjoy, starting with Barrel Proof. Housed in a nondescript building close to the interstate with only a small sign out front, it is easy to miss. Once you enter, you'll find a large bar and a decent number of tables. The whiskey list is well north of 300 bottles. Even though I don't think of it as a beer bar, they offer more than 30 selections.

You won't mistake Barrel Proof as a fancy place for cocktails, but the bartenders make as good a drink as any in the city. You'll be surrounded by locals, especially during happy hour when the drink of choice is the $6 old-fashioned. If you are a bourbon enthusiast, Barrel Proof is a must.

The Vintage (thevintagenola.com; 3121 Magazine St.; 504-324-7144) is an odd place but in a good way. It's technically a bar but has a French cafe vibe. At some tables you can order champagne by pressing a doorbell. The thing that takes it to a new level for me is that they also make and sell very good beignets, including beignet bites, which I have not seen on other menus. I would never have considered pairing beignets with champagne until I visited the Vintage, but I'm a convert.

The Vintage feels like a perfect first-date kind of place, or a fun spot to stop in after exploring busy Magazine Street. If you've already eaten at one of the many nearby restaurants, it's also a good place to have dessert and a nightcap. During the day it's a good spot with kids, especially if mom and dad need a drink while the kids get their boost of energy from the beignets.

Urban South (urbansouthbrewery.com; 1645 Tchoupitoulas St.; 504-267-4852) features a large number of brews and often releases new ones. The brewery and taproom are in a warehouse spacious enough for a dozen or more long picnic tables, a game area, an event space, pop-up food vendors, and a bounce house for the kids on weekends.

Courtyard Brewery (courtyardbrewery.square.site; 1160 Camp St.) is a nanobrewery focused on saisons and IPAs. At the time I wrote this, the menu had 13 offerings including a cherry pie sour, a saison with hibiscus, and something called an oyster stout. I had a key lime beer here once that I've never forgotten. One was enough, but it tasted exactly like the dessert, complete with hints of graham cracker crust. I still don't know how they did it.

SEE & DO

You can easily spend an afternoon or more exploring the oak-lined trees of the Garden District. If you add in shopping along Magazine Street, consider making a day of it.

The **St. Charles Avenue streetcar** (green) line (norta.com) dates back to 1835 and is the oldest continuously operating streetcar line in the world. It is the best way to get from Downtown to the Garden District, Uptown, or the Carrollton/Riverbend neighborhood.

The streetcar is a destination in itself and a great way to glimpse the grandeur of the Garden District. You can ride it to Audubon Park, Riverbend, or the end of the line at S. Claiborne Avenue. There is no air-conditioning on the green line but the windows open, which makes it perfect when the weather is nice.

It costs $1.25 each way (exact change only) to ride the streetcar at the time of this writing, or you can buy a Jazzy Pass for unlimited rides

(1-, 3-, 5-, or 31-day options available). Jazzy Passes are available in a magnetic card format, as well as on the RTA's Le Pass app (norta.com/ride-with-us/how-to-pay/lepass). The Le Pass app is the way to go if you plan on frequent rides and/or have multiple people in your group, since the app can be used to pay for everyone at once.

For more on the history of the streetcar in New Orleans, check out episode 16 of the *Beyond Bourbon Street* podcast.

The best way to learn about the Garden District is to either wander around on your own or take a guided tour. If you go it alone, you'll see what is said to be the largest collection of mansions in the United States. The architectural details make this area a playground for photographers and Instagrammers. Many of the homes have plaques on the iron fence out front describing the history of the home, the architect, and the home's significance in New Orleans history.

Lower Garden District mansion **MARK BOLOGNA**

Dual streetcars in the barn **MARK BOLOGNA**

MARGARET PLACE PARK

Margaret Place Park (1100 Margaret Place) is a tiny wedge of a park that honors Margaret Haughery, known as the mother of the orphans. Margaret's statue was put into place in 1884. It was the first one to honor a female on public land in the United States and the only one known to honor a baker.

Margaret was an Irish immigrant who came to America with her parents and settled in Baltimore. When she was nine, her parents died as a result of a yellow fever epidemic in 1822. In October 1835 Margaret married another Irish immigrant, Charles Haughery. They left Baltimore soon after and landed in New Orleans.

Charles was not well and soon traveled to Ireland. He took sick and eventually died. Not long after, their daughter Frances also died. At 23, Margaret was once again alone. She worked as a laundress in New Orleans, but soon decided to give a portion of her earnings to the Sisters of Charity to help orphans.

Margaret turned out to have a knack for business. She purchased a couple of dairy cows and sold the extra milk via milk cart, and over time grew the business. Within a couple of years she had 40 cows! Margaret continued to do all she could to help the nuns and the kids, giving them most of her earnings.

But she wasn't done. At some point, Margaret started working for a bakery. She loaned the owner money and eventually took over operations. Her bakery business soon became more successful than the dairy, and became her primary business. With no experience, she grew the bakery into a major operation and eventually the largest bakery in the United States.

When Margaret died at age 69 in 1882, she left $13,000 to six orphanages and two asylums for widows. That's over $300,000 in today's dollars. She also left a little over $50,000, or $1.2 million in today's dollars, to the Sisters of Charity.

Most people will get the best out of their time by taking a guided tour. Tours of the Garden District typically include the neighborhood as well as Lafayette Cemetery #1 across the street from Commander's Palace. *Note:* You can no longer enter the cemetery, but tour guides will take you to the gates where you'll have a good view of the above-ground crypts.

Two Chicks Walking Tours (twochickswalkingtours.com; 504-975-4386) is one of my favorite walking tour companies. Their knowledgeable guides will show you the homes, tell you about their famous residents past and present, and answer your questions about the neighborhood. One of the things I really like about Two Chicks is they limit the group size to no more than 12 people. Some of the other companies have far larger groups, which can lead to an impersonal experience.

While we are focused on the Garden District in this section, Two Chicks offers several different tours of the French Quarter and St. Louis Cemetery #1. *Full disclosure:* Christine Miller's Two Chicks is a longtime sponsor of the *Beyond Bourbon Street* podcast. However, they sponsor the show because I actively recruited them. I did so because of my enjoyment of their tours as well as my appreciation for the way Christine runs her company and the care she shows for her employees.

Lower Garden District balcony **MARK BOLOGNA**

The Garden District should be a must on your visit to New Orleans. While Bourbon Street may be the most famous, the grandeur of this area when combined with the huge live oak trees makes it a special place. On a more somber note, it is also important because underlying these grand structures is the fact that the businesses that financed them were built largely on the backs of the enslaved. All of it is a part of New Orleans history, and visiting this area helps to complete your view of the Crescent City.

Lower Garden District mansion **MARK BOLOGNA**

IRISH CHANNEL

The first Irish immigrants to come to New Orleans arrived during the Spanish Colonial period. During this time people left Ireland largely because of political reasons, and specifically to avoid English persecution. They generally headed to France or Spain to escape English domination, and to practice their Catholic faith. For similar reasons, some of these Irish citizens were attracted to New Orleans.

In the early to mid 1800s, a second, much larger wave of Irish immigrants came to New Orleans. Looking to escape the famine in their homeland, many found passage on the cotton ships. These ships left from New Orleans and traveled to Liverpool, where they dropped off their bales of cotton. In need of ballast for the return voyage, they were often filled with immigrants, many of Irish background.

By 1850, one in five New Orleanians was from Ireland. The largest concentration of Irish immigrants eventually settled in an area known as the Irish Channel. At the time, the Irish Channel was outside the city limits, in an area known as Lafayette City. This is not the Lafayette we know today in southwestern Louisiana. Rather, this was a city that encompassed parts of the present-day Garden District and the Irish Channel.

The current borders of the Irish Channel, like so much about New Orleans, are a little fuzzy depending on who you ask, but they basically run along the river to Magazine Street and from Jackson Avenue to Toledano Street.

EAT

I am only listing a couple of places here mainly because the Irish Channel is boxed in by the Garden District and Lower Garden District, which contain plenty of great places to eat. No matter which of the three neighborhoods you are in, you'll find plenty of options on or just off Magazine Street.

The Rum House (therumhouse.com; 3128 Magazine St.; 504-941-7560) is a good spot for families despite the name. The taco menu is described as Caribbean inspired, but the fried oyster tacos as well as the glazed shrimp hint at a New Orleans influence. The Rum House gets crowded during peak hours.

The Ruby Slipper Cafe (rubybrunch.com; 2802 Magazine St.; 504-525-9355) is a local chain of restaurants known for their big breakfasts. This location is easy to miss with all the nearby shops, but don't make that mistake. Call ahead to get on the wait list during peak hours, then enjoy the menu of omelettes, eggs Benedict variations, and specials.

DRINK

Parasol's (2533 Constance St.; 504-354-9079) is a dive bar, though new ownership spruced up the place a couple of years ago. It remains a popular corner bar, with po-boys on the menu and lots of TVs for watching Saints games and other sports.

On St. Patrick's Day the block of Third Street from Constance to Magazine becomes the center of New Orleans. In addition to a Mardi Gras–style parade, a raucous crowd fills up the street starting mid-morning. When St. Patrick's Day falls on a weekday, the crowd is full of people wearing work clothes, having left their Central Business District offices early to enjoy the party.

The Tchoup Yard Patio Bar (tchoupyard.com; 405 Third St.). Five streets behind Parasol's, the Tchoup Yard property takes up nearly a full square block, including ample off-street parking, rare in this part of town. There is a large patio with an open-air bar and plenty of seating. When it's too hot or raining, head inside, where there is plenty of space and a larger bar. The food is typical but very good bar fare, cooked up by Karibu Kitchen in a corner of the indoor space.

Miel Brewery and Taproom (mielbrewery.com; 405 Sixth St.; 504-372-4260) is a small craft brewery whose taproom flows between indoor and outdoor spaces. It has a neighborhood bar feel to it and is a hidden gem. Every time I've been to Miel, people are playing board games, sitting with dogs at their feet, and acting like they show up every day—maybe they do!

The menu typically includes 8 to 10 beers, all brewed in-house. Early on they were focused on sours, but over time the styles of beer covered here have grown. I find the best way to explore their menu is to get one or more flights of beer so you can sample the range. They often have a food truck out front, and during crawfish season, you can get a platter of boiled crawfish to go with your beer.

NOLA Brewing (nolabrewing.com; 3001 Tchoupitoulas St.; 504-896-9996) is one of the largest craft breweries in the New Orleans area. The taproom has plenty of tables and an upstairs covered balcony area. There are also picnic tables outside the brewery.

The draft menu changes as new beers are released and is updated on the digital screens behind the bar. You can expect to find offerings running the full range of beer styles, from a light lager to my favorite, the Irish Channel Stout. At the time of this writing the menu listed 23 different beers, so there is certain to be something you'll enjoy.

The Bulldog (draftfreak.com; 3236 Magazine St.; 504-891-1516) has more than 50 beers on tap and another 100 or so in bottles and cans. It is way too crowded for my taste during peak hours, but late on a hot summer afternoon the patio is a good place for a break and a beer.

SEE & DO

The part of Magazine Street that goes through the Lower Garden District and bisects the Garden District and the Irish Channel is rife with shopping opportunities. In addition to the bars and restaurants mentioned above, you'll encounter dozens of shops in this area ranging from local T-shirts (NOLA T-Shirt of the Month Club, Fleurty Girl), bakeries (Sucré, Haydel's), antiques stores and secondhand shops, art galleries, furniture stores, boutiques of all variety, and more.

If you love to shop, you'll enjoy Magazine Street. If you aren't a shopper but are traveling with someone who is, I offer this option, which is my favorite approach: either barhop your way along and leapfrog your partner while they shop, or get a drink to go from one of the bars and simply sit outside each spot while your mate does the browsing. Many places have benches or rocking chairs on the porch, presumably for this reason. I can't stand to shop but love visiting Magazine Street using this approach.

TOURO & EAST RIVERSIDE

These two neighborhoods combined are bordered by Toledano Street on the downtown side, St. Charles Avenue on the lake side, Napoleon as you continue towards Uptown, and Tchoupitoulas by the river. Touro, named for the large hospital that dominates this area, sits "above" East Riverside, with Magazine Street as the dividing line between the two. Most New Orleanians don't make a distinction.

For your purposes, what you need to know is this area is a sort of bridge between the Garden District and Uptown. The four main streets we discussed earlier (St. Charles, Prytania, Magazine, and Tchoupitoulas) continue as the main arteries and points of interest.

EAT

Atchafalaya (atchafalayarestaurant.com; 901 Louisiana Ave.; 504-891-9626) is a small restaurant tucked into a quiet corner off the beaten path. Serving brunch and dinner, the menu includes New Orleans

Touro cityscape **MARK BOLOGNA**

staples like gumbo and pan-sautéed trout but also inventive takes like the roast beef "Pao-boy" and duck confit with andouille sausage and sweet potatoes. The bright dining room is filled with artwork and features live music. This is a fairly casual restaurant, but reservations are recommended.

Mahony's Po-Boys (mahonyspoboys.com; 3454 Magazine St.; 504-899-3374) is your spot for the famous New Orleans sandwich along this stretch of Magazine Street. Occupying an old house, you can sit inside, on the front porch, or at one of the covered tables out front.

The po-boy list contains many that you would find across New Orleans, including roast beef, fried seafood (shrimp, oysters, or catfish), hot sausage, and ham, to name a few. What makes Mahony's distinctive are the other less common po-boys like the alligator sausage and the fried green tomato with pimento cheese. If you would prefer a plate lunch, you can expect New Orleans dishes like gumbo, crawfish étouffée, red beans and rice, and Crawfish Monica—a dish of Louisiana crawfish tails in a creamy sauce served over rotini pasta. This last dish is one of the most popular served at the annual New Orleans Jazz & Heritage Festival.

Mahoney's is casual, but prices are a bit higher than other neighborhood restaurants of a similar style. It's still a good choice while wandering this part of Magazine Street.

Imperial Woodpecker Sno-Balls (iwsnoballs.com; 3511 Magazine St.; 504-264-7170) makes their own flavors, which is what sets the best sno-ball stands apart. You'll find more than 40 flavors on the menu, but my favorite is wild strawberry. It's the best version of this flavor in the city and a perfect sugary treat on a hot summer day.

CR Coffee Shop (crcoffeenola.com; 3618 Magazine St.; 504-354-9422). If you prefer a cup of coffee over a sno-ball, we can't be friends. Seriously, though, CR Coffee Shop makes great coffee roasted locally. Owner Kevin Pedeaux takes great pride in his coffee, and it shows in the end product. What makes this spot nice besides the product is the small side-yard with cozy picnic tables—a good spot for the digital nomad to get work done, a business meeting, or just taking a break.

Lilette (liletterestaurant.com; 3637 Magazine St.; 504-895 1636) is in the group of restaurants I mentioned in the Garden District chapter when describing Coquette. Lilette is a cozy space that includes an outdoor patio and a menu that is inventive and approachable—perfect for an elegant dinner.

You'll find appetizers including grilled beets, burrata, and gnocchi. The entrée menu tends to have about four to six dishes and at the time of this writing included a duck breast, lamb shoulder, hanger steak, and a couple of fish dishes.

What this (and the others in this group) is not is a classic New Orleans eatery. If you are looking for gumbo, étouffée, or similar local dishes, look elsewhere. Reservations required.

La Petite Grocery (lapetitegrocery.com; 4238 Magazine St.; 504-891-3377) is led by James Beard Award–winning Chef Justin Devillier and his wife, Mia. This definitely falls into the gourmet dining category, though even less adventurous eaters will find something on the menu. My biggest complaint is that this is the kind of restaurant that serves smaller portions, which are probably closer to what we should all be eating, but I tend to want more. Regardless, if you love upscale dining and are looking for a high-end experience, La Petite Grocery fits the bill.

Shaya (shayarestaurant.com; 4213 Magazine St.; 504-891-4213) focuses on Israeli food. Locals, including me, rave about the hummus. They offer a few different varieties, all of which are delicious. Reservations recommended.

Casamento's (casamentosrestaurant.com; 4330 Magazine St.; 504-895-9761) has been serving fresh raw oysters since 1919. While oysters are the highlight of this small restaurant, you'll find plenty of other seafood dishes on the menu. Cash only.

Barracuda (eatbarracuda.com; 3984 Tchoupitoulas St.; 504-266-2961) is a taco stand with plenty of seating at picnic tables in the backyard. A good stop for lunch if you've been drinking at nearby Port Orleans Brewing Company and need some nourishment.

DRINK

Delachaise Wine Bar (3442 St. Charles Ave.; 504-895-0858) is a narrow bar that also includes outdoor tables where you can enjoy a glass of one of many wines while watching the streetcars go by. Popular with locals, this would be a good place to hop off the streetcar and enjoy a drink. The bar menu is eclectic and includes items like frog legs, eggplant cannoli, and a lamb burger.

The Columns Hotel (thecolumns.com; 3811 St. Charles Ave.; 504-899-9308) is a hotel, but the real draw is having a drink while sitting on the large front porch. I highly recommend taking a break from the streetcar to do just that. In the evening you'll often find live music in one of the front two parlors. In the bar itself are cozy spots to catch up with a friend or relive your visit while sipping a classic New Orleans cocktail. During Mardi Gras, patrons buy passes to access the grounds and the restrooms while enjoying the parades that pass by on the other side of St. Charles Avenue.

I'm showing my age, but the Columns was featured in 1978's *Pretty Baby*, starring 12-year-old Brooke Shields.

Bouligny Tavern (boulignytavern.com; 3641 Magazine St.; 504-891-1810). Back on Magazine Street, this bar sits across from Lilette. Small plates pair with cocktails and a decent list of wines by the glass. The space is cozy and elegant.

SEE & DO

Tipitina's (tipitinas.com; 501 Napoleon Ave.; 504-895-8477) is the best-known music venue in New Orleans, and with good reason. For decades many of the best bands locally and with wider reputations have played here. The name of the venue comes from a Professor Longhair song. If you enjoy live music and there is a performance at Tipitina's while you are in town, put it on your list.

Mardi Gras parades that use the Uptown route begin in one of two places. The first is this spot by Tipitina's. The second is at Jefferson and Magazine farther Uptown. Those parades intersect Napoleon at Magazine then mirror the route down St. Charles Avenue. On Mardi Gras day, parades come from S. Claiborne Avenue down Napoleon to St. Charles and therefore miss the river side of Napoleon all together.

I mention this because Napoleon as well as the first mile or so down St. Charles headed back towards the French Quarter are probably the most family-friendly parts of the parade routes. It is where we take our children and where I went to the parades as a young child with my parents.

Peaches Records (peachesrecordsandtapes.com; 4318 Magazine St.; 504-282-3322) is an old-school record shop with plenty of vinyl. The store is housed in an old Woolworth's diner, and they have kept the lunch counter in place to honor that memory, including the 1960s sit-ins that happened here and at other Woolworth locations.

UPTOWN

Once you cross Napoleon Avenue, you've entered Uptown New Orleans. In the widest definition of boundaries, Uptown refers to nearly a third of the city. For our purposes we'll use Tchoupitoulas Street, S. Claiborne Avenue, Audubon Park, and Napoleon. This also encompasses Tulane and Loyola Universities, so that area is sometimes called the University neighborhood.

St. Charles turns more residential the farther you go, which is one of the reasons I recommend the streetcar so highly. Taking it from Canal Street at the edge of the French Quarter and continuing all the way to the end of the line at S. Claiborne Avenue really gives you an appreciation for this part of New Orleans and how it changes as you go along.

EAT

Gautreau's (gautreausrestaurant.com; 1728 Soniat St.; 504-504-7397) is located a couple of blocks to the lake side of St. Charles Avenue. Don't try to find it by sight alone, since there is no sign out front. The only hint this is a restaurant are the large plate-glass windows, though they are shrouded by curtains. Inside you'll find a sophisticated and intimate restaurant favored by locals for a nice meal. Those who go tend to be regulars.

The menu leans towards French, as evidenced by the appetizers, which include sea scallops, beef tartare, foie gras, and duck confit. The entrées include Louisiana fish, duck, chicken, and a filet mignon. A perfect spot for a date night or special occasion, Gautreau's is definitely off the beaten path and a destination where you'll feel like you are in on a local secret.

Creole Creamery (creolecreamery.com; 4924 Prytania St.; 504-894-8680). This local ice-cream shop has about 18 regular flavors on the menu in addition to an ever-changing set of 6 or more specials that come and go throughout the year. The kids are partial to cotton candy, which tastes amazingly like the real thing, and to lavender honey. I like the café au lait.

Gracious Bakery (graciousbakery.com; 4930 Prytania St.; 504-300-8135). If you need coffee or a pastry, this bakery is in the same block as Creole Creamery. This location has a small courtyard out back in addition to ample seating inside.

La Crepe Nanou (lacrepenanou.com; 1410 Robert St.; 504-899-2670). This nearby French bistro and crêperie is a romantic spot that will remind diners of Paris.

St. James Cheese Company (stjamescheese.com; 5400 Prytania St.; 504-899-4737). Continuing into the next block of Prytania Street is the St. James Cheese Company, the sister to the Warehouse District location. This is a popular spot and includes a menu of sandwiches, salads, and cheese plates, making it an excellent choice for a lighter lunch.

Magazine Street continues to offer a lot of options in Uptown, as it does in other parts of its travels from the Central Business District.

La Boulangerie (laboulangerienola.com; 4600 Magazine St.; 504-269-3777) makes excellent breads and pastries. During Carnival they make the *galette des rois*, a version of king cake more common in France. Instead of a brioche-based oval cake, the *galette des rois* is an almond paste–filled flaky pie. In addition to king cakes and pastries, La Boulangerie is a solid choice for a light lunch of salad and sandwich.

Pizza Domenica (pizzadomenica.com; 4993 Magazine St.; 504-301-4978) serves pizza cooked in a custom-made Italian oven. The dining room is always bustling and tends to lean younger and hip.

Tito's Ceviche and Pisco (titoscevichepisco.com; 5015 Magazine St.; 504-267-7612) is a small restaurant serving authentic Peruvian food. The ceviche shrimp is my favorite appetizer, followed by the *lomo saltado* (tenderloin tips) as a main course. As the name implies, pisco cocktails are the focus, and they do a fine job. This spot makes for a quiet dinner or a nice place to meet up for drinks and small plates.

Guy's Po-Boys (5259 Magazine St.; 504-891-5025) is one of two exceptional po-boy shops in this part of town (keep reading to learn about the other). No frills and cash only, Guy's consistently serves up delicious classics like roast beef and fried shrimp. The fried shrimp are plentiful and crispy. One full-sized po-boy and an order of fries is plenty for two people to easily share.

Saba (eatwithsaba.com; 5757 Magazine St.; 504-324-7770) is the newest creation from Chef Alon Shaya. Earlier I mentioned the restaurant Shaya, which was Alon's first restaurant and still bears his name. After a split among ownership, Chef Shaya took his talents and his focus on Israeli cuisine Uptown to open Saba. You'll find a similar menu here, anchored by several versions of hummus. Saba is bright and lively, with gorgeous indoor spaces and umbrella-covered tables outdoors for beautiful days.

Avo (restaurantavo.com; 5908 Magazine St.; 504-509-6550), whose name means "grandfather" or "ancestor," serves regional Italian food and is led by native New Orleanian Chef Nick Lama. The menu includes standard Italian fare as well as a few more-adventurous plates like charred octopus. In 2020 the restaurant underwent a major renovation, and the result is an intimate dining space perfect for a night out.

Taqueria Corona (taqueriacorona.com; 5932 Magazine St.; 504-897-3974) opened in 1988 with the idea of serving authentic Mexican food in a casual environment. It worked and nearly 40 years later, locals in this part of town know Taqueria Corona as a family-friendly and inexpensive place for no-frills Mexican food. I've been coming to this location since it first opened and have watched it evolve and grow while staying true to the original vision of owner Roberto Méndez.

Reginelli's Pizzeria (reginellis.com; 5961 Magazine St.; 504-899-1414) is one of a small chain of local pizza shops. This one, in the heart of Uptown, is very popular with families. It could be because of the happy hour, providing parents with cheap drinks while the kids eat an early dinner. In addition to the traditional toppings you would expect on a pizza, there are some unique varieties, including the gumbo pizza with andouille sausage, shrimp, and okra, and the Frescanon with artichokes and feta. You'll find us here a couple of times per month.

Picnic Provisions and Whiskey (nolapicnic.com; 741 State St.; 504-266-2810). Across the street from Reginelli's, the name implies that the menu focuses on items that would make for a nice picnic on the nearby riverfront, though there is seating inside and out. You'll find small plates like pimento cheese, crab dip, boudin egg rolls, and crab and corn beignets, as well as sandwiches and even a couple of lunch plates. This is a different take on the New Orleans restaurant, but they pull it off very well.

Domilise's Po-Boys (domilisespoboys.com; 5240 Annunciation St.; 504-899-9126) is the "other" po-boy shop I referenced when writing about Guy's earlier. Domilise's has a loyal following of regulars as well as people who make the pilgrimage on every visit to the city. Good thing, because you have to know what you're looking for to find it. The only clue you've arrived at the right place is the small hand-painted sign over the corner door.

It doesn't look like much from the outside or the inside, but since sometime around 1920 they've been serving drinks and sandwiches that people keep coming back for. A fried shrimp po-boy is the go-to choice, but the menu includes others like roast beef, ham, and hot sausage. Students from nearby Tulane and Loyola Universities get 20 percent off on Tuesdays and Thursdays, ensuring future generations of customers.

Frankie & Johnny's (frankieandjohnnys.net; 321 Arabella St.; 504-243-1234) was opened in 1942 to serve large plates of seafood to the nearby workers along the docks on the Mississippi River. They continue the tradition today, offering big plates of seafood and other New Orleans dishes to workers, families, and visitors. When I think of Frankie & Johnny's, I think of boiled crawfish during springtime.

Clancy's (clancysneworleans.com; 6100 Annunciation St.; 504-895-1111) is my wife's favorite neighborhood restaurant. This fact nearly derailed our courtship when she announced it to my entire family while sitting in the neighborhood restaurant *we owned* (not Clancy's) at the time. My mom looked up at me and said, "I don't think this is going to work out." Fortunately it did, because here we are more than two decades later.

INSIDER TIP: Take an Uber or a Lyft. Clancy's is nestled in a residential neighborhood and is easy to miss if you don't know exactly where it is.

In any event, Clancy's is our go-to spot for date night, anniversaries, and more. It is the classic New Orleans bistro. I can't walk in without knowing someone, which is a sure sign it is a place for locals.

Clancy's is a neighborhood restaurant in that it is nestled in a residential area and primarily caters to locals who eat there on a regular basis. The food and the service are more upscale than the typical New Orleans neighborhood restaurant, with white tablecloths and servers in tuxedos. Even with that nod to formality, Clancy's still comes across as laid back.

Sit downstairs to be in the middle of it all, or ask for a table upstairs for a quiet conversation. Start with the fried oysters and brie or the turtle soup. I love the Veal Annunciation as a main course, though any of the fish specials will be fresh and well prepared. Save room for dessert and get the homemade peppermint ice cream.

Hansen's Sno-Bliz (snobliz.square.site; 4801 Tchoupitoulas St.; 504-891-9788) is the granddad of New Orleans sno-balls and has been a local tradition since the 1930s. If you've been to Hawaii and had a shave ice, the texture is very similar. Don't call it a snow cone—it's not the same. The difference is the ice. A sno-ball is not crunchy, and it doesn't come in a cone.

If you want to watch a New Orleanian's head explode, ask them where to get a snow cone. *Disclaimer:* I am not responsible for anything that happens after you utter those words!

Hansen's was started by Ernest and Mary Hansen in the 1930s when Ernest built the first ice-shaving machine. Two of his earliest machines are still used today. The extremely popular stand is run by Ashley Hansen, one of Mary and Ernest's grandchildren. Ashley continues the tradition of quality and hard work.

Hansen's **JAMES CULLEN**

All flavors are made in-house, and combined with the texture of the ice created by Ernest's machines, there is no comparable sno-ball in New Orleans. Lines are long but worth the wait at this New Orleans institution. Highly recommended.

The most popular area for casual dining on the lake side of St. Charles Avenue is Freret Street, particularly the stretch from Napoleon Avenue to Jefferson Street. You'll find more than a dozen restaurants, a couple of bars, and some small shops.

High Hat Cafe (highhatcafe.com; 4500 Freret St.; 504-754-1336) is a casual restaurant focused on Southern food. They pride themselves on fresh catfish and shrimp, though my favorite dishes include the slow-roasted pork, the fried chicken, and the smoky chicken and sausage gumbo. Off the beaten path for most tourists, High Hat is perfect for lunch or a casual dinner.

Ice Cream 504 (icecream504.com; 2511 Jena St.; 504-266-2708) is that rare place offering homemade ice cream with fresh ingredients and New Orleans sno-balls. It is tucked a half block off Freret in a nondescript building and is often overlooked. Don't make that mistake if you've decided to explore this area.

The Company Burger (thecompanyburger.com; 4600 Freret St.; 504-267-0320) has a menu that features one of the best burgers in town paired with fresh onion rings, fries, or tater tots. They also serve an underappreciated fried chicken sandwich. Kid friendly.

Val's (valsnola.com; 4632 Freret St.; 504-356-0006) took the place of an old gas station and immediately became a hit among locals for their tacos, queso, and outdoor space.

Dat Dog (datdog.com; 5030 Freret St.; 504-899-6883). Like it's siblings in the Marigny and the Garden District, Dat Dog serves up sausages and hot dogs along with a decent selection of draft beer. This location has a large outdoor seating area that's covered, making it a good spot even during those hot summer days.

DRINK

Le Bon Temps Roule (lbtrnola.com; 4801 Magazine St.; 504-897-3448) is an iconic corner bar that features live music and free oysters on Fridays.

Henry's Uptown Bar (5101 Magazine St.; 504-324-8140) is a corner dive bar that's been serving the neighborhood for more than 100 years. Henry's sits along the parade route for many Mardi Gras parades. Popular with locals all year long, they claim to have the coldest beer in town, with more than 50 varieties on the menu. A great place to enjoy a beer, have some bar food, and mix with the locals.

Cure (curenola.com; 4905 Freret St.; 504-302-2357) is one of the best cocktail bars in New Orleans and has been named one of the best bars in America by both *Esquire* and *Food & Wine*. While locals know Cure as a great spot for cocktails and light bites, it is easy to miss. There is no sign on the building, which is housed in an old fire station. If you are into craft cocktails, put this one on your list. Plan on a casual meal at one of the nearby eateries, then head to Cure for an evening of drinks.

SEE & DO

The primary attraction in this part of town is **Audubon Park.** New Orleans is home to magnificent live oak trees, and two of the best places to wander among them are City Park and Audubon Park.

Audubon is accessible via the St. Charles streetcar line and features a nearly 2-mile walking path, huge live oak trees, a golf course, several playgrounds for children, and the **Audubon Zoo** (audubonnatureinstitute.org/zoo; 6500 Magazine St.; 504-861-2537). The grounds encompassing the park were also the site of the 1884 World's Industrial and Cotton Centennial.

Behind the zoo is an area known to locals as **"The Fly"** for a large structure on the grounds. The Fly is along the Mississippi River batture and is an excellent spot to enjoy the sunset and the river traffic. You'll

see people grouped together on picnic blankets enjoying a bottle of wine, playing Frisbee with their dogs, and generally enjoying life in New Orleans.

Octavia Books (octaviabooks.com; 513 Octavia St.; 504-899-7323) is my favorite bookstore in New Orleans when it comes to looking for books about New Orleans. This is my go-to spot when researching topics for the podcast. I know I can ask the staff for recommendations on my topic and they will always deliver.

RIVERBEND/CARROLLTON

The Carrollton neighborhood encompasses several subdistricts including Riverbend, Black Pearl, Fontainebleau, Broadmoor, Holly Grove, and Gert Town. We'll cover them all here with the exception of Broadmoor, which has its own chapter. Bounded by Broadway, the Orleans Parish–Jefferson Parish line, Earhart Boulevard, and Tchoupitoulas Street, the area offers plenty of restaurants, the continuation of the streetcar line, and quiet residential areas to explore.

I like the Riverbend area so much that I did an early episode of the *Beyond Bourbon Street* podcast about it (beyondbourbonst.com/21). Some of the restaurants mentioned in the podcast are no longer with us but most are, and the recording will give you some depth and history about the area that I can't cover here.

EAT

Brigtsen's (brigtsens.com; 723 Dante St.; 504-862-7610). This brilliant Creole bistro is tucked into the Riverbend neighborhood and is one of my two or three favorite restaurants in New Orleans. If you like rabbit,

Fleur-de-lis mural MARK BOLOGNA

Brigtsen's is a must. Similarly, any dish with duck or fish is going to be a winner. I typically order the double-cut pork chop, but trust your server and order what they tell you to. The menu is not large, but everything is fresh. Make reservations. Highly recommend.

Note: Chef Frank Brigtsen worked alongside Chef Paul Prudhomme at Commander's Palace in the 1970s, and later at K-Paul's. Chef Frank is truly one of the most caring and entertaining chefs in the business. Tell him I sent you. (Listen to episode 38 of the *Beyond Bourbon Street* podcast to hear my discussion with Chef Frank.)

Tartine (tartineneworleans.com; 7217 Perrier St.; 504-855-4860) is a French patisserie, offering a light breakfast, sandwiches, quiche, and sweets.

Camellia Grill (camelliagrillnola.com; 626 S. Carrollton Ave.; 504-309-2679) is a New Orleans institution that has been serving straightforward breakfast, burgers, and desserts since 1946. When it closed after Hurricane Katrina, local residents plastered the front doors with messages pleading with them to reopen. Ultimately this drive was successful, and Camellia once again opened to serve locals and visitors alike. *Note:* The line gets long and meanders down the street during peak hours.

Empanola (empanolaempanadas.com; 7321 Freret St.; 504-249-5977) offers empanadas with a New Orleans twist. These include the gumbo (my favorite) and crawfish, as well as more-standard versions with chorizo or ham and cheese. They have a daily special with two empanadas and a salad that is my go-to lunch when I am in this part of town. I get it to go and sit out on the batture behind Audubon Park.

INSIDER TIP: Empanola is a perfect lunch spot for Tulane students or parents who are visiting.

Vincent's Italian Cuisine (vincentsitaliancuisine.com; 7839 St. Charles Ave.; 504-866-93113) is a cozy restaurant serving New Orleans Italian (which is to say influenced by Sicilian and New Orleans flavors) dishes. Somehow it manages to be both kid friendly and a good place for date night. Reservations recommended for weekend dining.

Louisiana Pizza Kitchen (louisianapizzakitchenuptown.com; 6515 S. Carrollton Ave.; 504-866-5900) has a large menu beyond pizza. The pizzas themselves are thin and crispy. They have the usual pizza toppings, plus locally influenced ones like the "three meat" with alligator and andouille sausage and the shrimp pizza. The rest of the menu is large and includes two of my favorites, fried eggplant parmesan and stuffed bell peppers. The portions are big and the place is casual, making it a good spot for families.

Williams Plum Street Snowballs (1300 Burdette St.). If you're riding the streetcar and suddenly have the urge for a snowball, hop off near Plum Street and walk a short couple of blocks to Williams Plum Street Snowballs. They've been serving more than 50 flavors of the sugary treat for decades. You open the screen door, step inside the tiny space, and order, before exiting through another screen door and waiting outside. There are a couple of benches, though many people get their snowball and walk around the neighborhood.

The Carrollton neighborhood has two streets worth exploring. The first is Maple Street, which runs parallel to St. Charles Avenue.

I mostly think of Maple as a street with breakfast options, including an outlet of **Satsuma Cafe** (satsumacafe.com; 7901 Maple St.; 504-309-5557) mentioned in the Bywater chapter of this book.

The second street to focus on is Oak Street. Walking down Oak feels like stepping back in time to a main street in a small town. You'll find coffee, restaurants, bars, shops, and more.

Rue De La Course (ruedelacourse.com; 1140 S. Carrollton Ave.; 504-861-4343) is an excellent coffee shop housed in a former bank building. The ample small tables and cozy spot upstairs are often filled with college students studying over a latte.

Cibo (cibonola.com; 1114 S. Carrollton Ave.; 504-592-7797). Around the corner on S. Carrollton Avenue, this tiny restaurant offers classic Italian sandwiches accompanied by pasta salad. The sandwiches are large and freshly prepared, making it a good place to keep in mind for lunch. I like the chicken parmesan sandwich, big enough to share.

Z'otz Cafe (zotzcafe.com; 8210 Oak St.; 504-861-2224). Back on Oak Street, you'll find this bohemian spot for tea and coffee.

Jacques-Imo's (jacques-imos.com; 8325 Oak St.; 504-861-0886). The food is much better than you might think, judging the place from the outside. You have to walk through the kitchen to get to the dining room, but don't let that deter you.

INSIDER TIP: Don't go during the big seasons like Mardi Gras and Jazz Fest, unless you leave early and beat the rush. Jacques-Imo's only takes reservations for groups of five or more, so expect to wait if you get there much after 6 p.m. They are closed in August.

Typically, the server will bring you fried oysters and a small salad as a complimentary starter. Try the fried grits if they are on the menu—sometimes crawfish, sometimes shrimp and tasso. I like the stuffed pork chop, made with ground beef, shrimp, and mushrooms and smothered with brown gravy. The menu is large and includes favorites like blackened redfish, swordfish, crawfish or shrimp étouffée, and fried green tomatoes.

Breads on Oak (breadsonoak.com; 8640 Oak St.; 504-324-8271) is an organic bakery with vegan and vegetarian options on the menu for breakfast and lunch.

Boureé (bourreenola.com; 1510 S. Carrollton Ave.; 504-510-4040) specializes in chicken wings and fresh fruit daiquiris. The inside isn't much, but the ample outdoor seating space is a nice place to relax and enjoy the food. They occasionally have live music.

Boucherie (boucherie-neworleans.com; 8115 Jeannette St.; 504-852-5114). Around the corner is Boureé's sophisticated sister, Boucherie. *Boucherie* refers to the Cajun tradition of butchering a whole hog for a family gathering. Housed in an old cottage, the menu is primarily focused on pork, beef, and fresh fish.

Riccobono's Panola Street Cafe (panolastreetcafe.com; 7801 Panola St.; 504-314-1810) is my neighborhood breakfast spot. Big breakfasts including a variety of omelettes and buttery biscuits are the way to go. I like to sit at the bar and chat with the lively crew of servers. Riccobono's reminds me of the neighborhood restaurant my parents owned when I was a kid. Most people who eat here are regulars.

DRINK

Cooter Brown's (cooterbrowns.com; 509 S. Carrollton Ave.; 504-866-9104) is an easy destination in Riverbend a half block from where the streetcar turns off St. Charles and onto S. Carrollton Avenue. Cooter's is known for its massive beer list of 400-plus beers as well as its raw oysters on the half shell. It is a favorite of students from nearby Loyola and Tulane but is a good spot for any lover of beer.

Oak Street Brewery (oakstbrewery.com; 8201 Oak St.; 504-533-9139) opened in late 2020 and is a friendly spot for dogs and children, not to mention beer-swilling patrons. Offering a dozen or so beers brewed in-house, I like the Mochachu dark stout and the Goofy Henry's Juicy English IPA.

Oak & Ale (oakandalenola.com; 8118 Oak St.; 504-302-1845) is two bars in one, sitting next to each other and sharing a courtyard. The wine bar has a nice selection of a dozen or so wines by the glass. They offer small plates to accompany the wine and have live music on weekends. The beer side typically has 30 or more beers on tap and better-than-expected pub food.

Maple Leaf Bar (mapleleafbar.com; 8316 Oak St.; 504-866-9359) is a funky and fun place for late-night music. Located next to Jacques-Imo's, patrons often load up on food there before heading over to the Maple Leaf for an 11 p.m. show. If you are in town on a Tuesday, catch Rebirth Brass Band for the late set.

Snake and Jake's Christmas Club Lounge (snakeandjakes.com; 7612 Oak St.; 504-861-2802) almost defies description. If you were visiting me and asked to go to the best dive bar in town, we would go to Snake and Jake's. Very easy to miss, it looks like a shack on a residential street. Inside the dimly lit bar, you'll find holiday decor and a good jukebox to go with friendly bartenders and a crowd of regulars. Snake and Jake's is known for its late hours and gets more crowded after 11 p.m.

Madigan's (800 S. Carrollton Ave.) was the bar we snuck into in high school to play pool and drink beer. Nearly 40 years later, I still go there to catch up with friends.

Carrollton Station (carrolltonstationnola.com; 8140 Willow St.; 504-865-9190) gets its name from the streetcar barn across the street. If the large doors are open, sneak a peek of the barn before heading into this corner bar. With indoor and outdoor seating, Carrollton Station is small but keeps a full calendar of events, including live music and trivia night.

Snake and Jake's MARK BOLOGNA

Ship on the river, batture view **MARK BOLOGNA**

SEE & DO

The levee is a popular spot to walk, run, or ride a bike. The grass between the levee and the road is popular for playing catch with dogs. You'll also see the occasional person on horseback riding from the stables about a mile upriver. For the adventurous, put on your waterproof boots and explore the batture, the wooded area between the levee and the river. You'll be rewarded with eye-level views of the river traffic and the barges tied up along the shore.

Oak Street Po-Boy Festival
MARK BOLOGNA

Once a year Oak Street is home to the aptly named **Oak Street Po-Boy Festival** (www.poboyfest.com). The dates move from year to year, but it is generally held on a November weekend when the New Orleans Saints are out of town.

The festival has a weird fee structure: free to get in, but $10 to get a wristband and then purchase po-boys at the booth. Don't let this deter you. There are lots of food options, including creative takes on the po-boy. In the past my favorite has been a BBQ shrimp po-boy, with the shrimp poured into the end of a loaf of French bread.

Several stages offer live music. It is one of our favorite neighborhood festivals, but it gets very crowded, so go early or late, especially if you have young children in strollers.

Rock N Bowl (rocknbowl.com; 3016 S. Carrollton Ave.; 504-861-1700) offers bowling and live music. The kids like to go during the daytime to bowl; the adults enjoy the consistently good schedule of local live music.

Southport Music Hall (southporthall.com; 200 Monticello St.; 504-835-2903) is just across the parish line into Jefferson. It originally opened in the early 1900s as an illegal casino, but by the 1960s it had become home to a local social organization. In the early 2000s it became a music hall offering two stages for live music. Check the schedule.

BROADMOOR

Broadmoor is a section of Carrollton/Uptown that has enough places that it is worth mentioning separately. All are gathered within a couple of blocks of each other and are really only accessible if you have a car or take a rideshare. I would not recommend this area at night, though others would surely disagree.

EAT & DRINK

Laurel Street Bakery (laurelstreetbakery.com; 2701 S. Broad St.; 504-897-0576) makes their own bagels in addition to standard breakfast fare. Lunch includes a solid array of sandwiches and salads. There is more seating than you would think from the outside.

El Pavo Real (elpavorealnola.com; 4401 S. Broad St.; 504-266-2022) offers classic Mexican dishes for breakfast, lunch, and dinner. Tucked into a small corner building, it is popular with neighborhood residents who know how good the food is.

MIDCITY & ESPLANADE AVENUE

As the name implies, the Midcity neighborhood covers a large swath in the middle of New Orleans. For our purposes I am going to expand the geographic boundaries by a couple of blocks. This will make it easier to talk about and easier for you to picture.

The riverside of Gentilly is bounded by S. Broad Street. I-10 is the Uptown boundary, Esplanade Avenue on the lake side (this is where I've taken some liberty), and City Park Avenue the uppermost. What you end up with is a shape similar to that of home plate on a baseball diamond. Esplanade runs from the river all the way to the front of City Park.

Midcity is mostly residential but includes Bayou St. John, plenty of restaurants, and St. Louis Cemetery #3. City Park is adjacent and sits between Midcity and Lakeview. Because there is so much to do in City Park, we'll cover it in its own section.

The easiest way to get to Midcity from Downtown and the French Quarter is the streetcar. Take the Canal Street line (red streetcar) headed away from the river. Make sure you are on the Carrollton/City Park extension. Ride it to the end at City Park, then hop off and explore the park, Bayou St. John, Esplanade Avenue, and St. Louis #3.

A note about the red streetcars: They are patterned after the green cars, but because they are not held to the same historical standards, there are a few differences. Most notably, they are air-conditioned! This comes with a cost, however, in that the windows cannot be opened.

EAT

You can hop on the streetcar and take it down Canal Street until the intersection with Carrollton Avenue. At that point the streetcar will turn right onto Carrollton. Just before you turn off Canal Street is Mandina's Restaurant.

Mandina's Restaurant (mandinasrestaurant.com; 3800 Canal St.; 504-482-9179). Since 1932 Mandina's has been serving New Orleanians with a classic menu including seafood, Italian dishes, po-boys, and gumbo. New Orleans is home to a large contingent of people of Sicilian descent, so Italian dishes are common, especially on the menus of neighborhood joints like Mandina's.

Neyow's Creole Cafe (neyows.com; 3332 Bienville St.; 504-827-5474). A few blocks before Carrollton Avenue, the streetcar will cross the Norman C. Francis Parkway. A couple of blocks to your right will be Neyow's, which features a large menu including po-boys, gumbo, fried chicken, pork chops, and daily specials that are filled with classic Creole/soul food selections like red beans or jambalaya (Mondays), white beans (Tuesdays), and mustard greens (Wednesdays).

Katie's (katiesinmidcity.com; 3701 Iberville St.; 504-488-6582) is not far away. It serves excellent New Orleans food in a classic neighborhood environment—a perfect spot for meeting a client, casual date night, or lunch with the kids!

Katie's is typical of a New Orleans neighborhood restaurant: corner shops that serve an excellent po-boy and a mixture of plate lunches and dinners, usually heavy on seafood and Italian. Many, but not all, serve alcohol. Katie's hits these marks spot-on, and adds just a bit of upscale-ness (is that a word?) to its menu. Maybe "inventiveness" is a better choice of words. Whatever, they do what they do well.

INSIDER TIP: I love Katie's chicken and andouille gumbo and the red beans and rice with hot sausage. I also like the fried shrimp po-boy. One of my frequent lunch partners always orders the Mama Mia Italian Salad. People swear by the Boudreaux pizza, too. Any of the specials with fish will be excellent! Their ribs are smoked across the street and feature a blackberry jalapeño BBQ sauce. Get the crawfish beignet as an appetizer and share it with a friend. If you don't care about calories, ask if they will fry it instead of baking it. Seriously.

Neighborhood places like Katie's are the reason why New Orleanians have never been fond of chain restaurants. We don't need 'em!

Once the streetcar turns onto Carrollton Avenue, you'll reach an area full of places to eat and drink. On your right just after the turn will be **Venezia's** (venezianeworleans.com; 134 N. Carrollton Ave.; 504-488-7991). This place has been around since 1957. *Full disclosure:* Venezia's is owned by my dad's cousin, but it is an institution with excellent pizza and a nice range of Italian dishes in a casual environment.

Another block down, also on the right, is **Angelo Brocato's** (angelo brocatoicecream.com; 214 N. Carrollton Ave.; 504-486-1465) ice-cream parlor. In business since 1905, they serve wonderful ice cream and Italian desserts, including some of the best cannoli I've ever eaten. I am also partial to their seed cookies if that is your thing.

While this is not the original location, it has been here for a while and is the only surviving parlor. It is like stepping back in time. I don't have much of a sweet tooth, but I cannot say no to their cannoli or Italian cookies.

Porgy's Seafood Market (porgysseafood.com; 236 N. Carrollton Ave.; 504-429-3474) serves boiled and fried seafood that varies with the season. They also are known for bycatch—that is, locally caught fish that might be outside of the norm. They will prepare anything in their fish case for you while you wait. Their locally caught shrimp and Des Allemands catfish po-boys are worth a stop.

Three blocks down Bienville Street is **Clesi Seafood** (clesicatering.com; 4323 Bienville St.; 504-909-0108), with a menu of boiled seafood and also with a few more New Orleans items.

As you continue down Carrollton in the direction of City Park, keep an eye out on your left. You'll soon come across **Pandora's Snowballs** (facebook.com/PandorasSnowballs; 901 N. Carrollton Ave.; 504-285-4867).

If you need more sustenance, head across the side street to **Toups Meatery** (toupsmeatery.com; 845 N. Carrollton Ave.; 504-252-4999). There you'll find a menu heavy on meat, as the name implies. Chef Isaac Toups was born in Rayne, Louisiana, in the heart of Cajun country. This heritage shows up on the menu, which often includes wild game, boudin, cracklins, and hog's head cheese. You can count on at least one Wagyu steak cut and a double-cut pork chop for the less adventurous. Toups is not your place if you or a member of your party is vegan or vegetarian.

Note: Isaac and Amanda Toups are also very active in the community, organizing an effort to feed thousands of schoolkids during the summer, when school lunch programs are not available.

Across Carrollton Avenue is **Blue Oak BBQ** (blueoakbbq.com; 900 N. Carrollton Ave.; 504-822-2583). I'm a big fan of their pepper-crusted brisket (ask for some of the fatty pieces), the smoked chicken wings with jerk sauce, and the spicy mac-n-cheese. When the weather is nice, sit at one of the communal picnic tables outside. If dining alone, I like the small indoor bar.

Across the street from Delgado Community College is **Ike's Snowballs** (520 City Park Ave.; 504-208-9983). This is our go-to snowball stand near City Park. There are plenty of flavors to choose from and lots of outdoor tables. Ike's also is open out of season, or at least longer than most of its counterparts.

Parkway Bakery & Tavern (parkwaypoorboys.com; 538 Hagan Ave.; 504-482-3047) is one of the most popular po-boy spots in New Orleans, with good reason. They first opened in 1911 and have been serving the neighborhood since then. Their roast beef po-boys along with the fried shrimp are two of my favorites. The line to order at the inside counter often snakes outside. Once you order you sit outside under large tents. Plenty of parking and also convenient if you are riding bikes along the Lafitte Greenway.

On Esplanade Avenue, **Cafe Degas** (cafedegas.com; 3127 Esplanade Ave.; 504-945-5635) is one of my favorite places on a cool evening or a Sunday morning for brunch. The ambience is great, and the food is excellent. This is a romantic place for dinner, or a great place to spend an evening in good conversation with friends.

INSIDER TIP: If you go to Cafe Degas for brunch, try the grillades and grits. For dinner, the onion soup followed by the hanger steak is my choice.

Most of the seating is outside on their covered patio, though they often drop the see-through shades and have plenty of AC or heat depending on the need. It's a white tablecloth place, though you are sitting on iron patio chairs. The cafe is named for the French Impressionist Edgar Degas, who had family in New Orleans and lived just down the street from here in 1872–1873.

To get there by streetcar, take the Canal Street line (the red one), Carrollton extension. Stay on it until the end of the line. The cost as of this writing is $1.25 each way, exact change. Hop off in front of City Park and walk down Esplanade Avenue. You'll cross Bayou St. John, then will see St. Louis Cemetery #3 on your left. Walk several more blocks and you'll come to Cafe Degas.

Liuzza's by the Track (liuzzasbtt.com; 1518 N. Lopez St.; 504-218-7888) is a neighborhood watering hole next door to the New Orleans Fairgrounds horse racing track. The fairgrounds also happens to be the site of the annual New Orleans Jazz & Heritage Festival, which means tens of thousands of people walk by Liuzza's on their way into the main gate. It's a popular stop for a Bloody Mary or a beer before heading into Jazz Fest or on the way out. The rest of the year it is a good spot for a po-boy or a fried seafood plate. If you go, get the BBQ shrimp po-boy.

Lola's (lolasneworleans.com; 3312 Esplanade Ave.; 504-488-6946) is a tiny restaurant offering authentic Spanish cuisine. The menu is large and includes tapas, soups, paella, and entrées featuring fish, duck, lamb, and pork.

DRINK

Bayou Beer Garden (bayoubeergarden.com; 326 Norman C. Francis Pkwy.; 504-302-9357) is located just off the Lafitte Greenway and offers plenty of outdoor seating, a large beer menu, and delicious boiled crawfish when in season. Adjacent to the beer garden is Bayou Wine Garden—equally popular, with a large wine list and the same food.

Revel (revelcafeandbar.com; 133 N. Carrollton Ave.; 504-309-6122) is owned by Chris McMillian, a cocktail historian who helped found the Museum of the American Cocktail and was named by *Imbibe* magazine as one of the 25 most influential people in the cocktail industry in the previous century. How's that for credentials? If you are in this part of New Orleans and are serious about cocktails, you'll want to stop in.

Finn McCool's Irish Pub (finnmccools.com; 3701 Banks St.; 504-486-9080) is the spot for soccer and rugby matches. Large crowds gather to cheer on their favorite teams from the English and Scottish Premier Leagues, the Champions League, and pretty much any sporting event. It was named one of the 10 best Irish bars in the world by the *Irish Times*.

Banks Street Bar (4401 Banks St.; 504-486-0258) features live entertainment almost every night to go with the cheap drinks in a neighborhood dive bar setting.

Second Line Brewing (secondlinebrewing.com; 433 N. Bernadotte St.; 504-248-8979) is Midcity's neighborhood craft brewery. Limited indoor seating, but they do have a pet- and child-friendly beer garden. The core menu typically includes five or six offerings as well as another three or four small-batch beers. They also offer five annual releases throughout the year.

Deutches Haus (deutscheshaus.org; 1700 Moss St.; 504-522-8014) sits along Bayou St. John and hosts a variety of events celebrating German culture. While it is a membership organization, the bar is open to anyone during operating hours.

SEE & DO

First and foremost is **City Park.** There is so much to do in the park, we'll cover it in the next chapter of this guide. Beyond that, I mentioned the **Lafitte Greenway** (lafittegreenway.org) in the section about the Tremé, but here in Midcity is the other end of this 2.6-mile linear park. It includes a bicycle trail, park space, playgrounds, and outdoor works of art. It was opened in 2015 and has become a popular place for New Orleanians to enjoy the outdoors.

The **Canal (red) streetcar line** is my recommended way of traveling from downtown New Orleans to Midcity, but it is also a fun thing to do in itself, even if you just ride and see the sights along the way. You have two options on this line. The first is described above: take the Carrollton extension and head towards City Park, Esplanade Avenue, and Bayou St. John.

Along **Bayou St. John** you'll find a walking path. For the most scenic part, go to the right and wander the path until it ends near Parkway Bakery. Along this stretch of the bayou, you will find the bright blue **Cabrini Bridge.** Nearby is the **Pitot House** (pitothouse.org; 1440 Moss St.; 504-482-0312), which houses a small museum and is a popular place for wedding receptions.

Bayou St. John played an important role in New Orleans history. Before the French founded the present city of New Orleans, the bayou was an important route for Indians, who called it Bayou Choupic. The French used this waterway and a nearby portage to travel from the Mississippi River though Lake Pontchartrain and to the site of the original city, the French Quarter. This route was much faster than traveling the 95 or so meandering miles from the Gulf of Mexico up the Mississippi River to the French Quarter riverfront.

If you cross Bayou St. John directly in front of City Park, you'll quickly come to **St. Louis Cemetery #3** (3421 Esplanade Ave.) on your left. While not the most popular, it is my favorite of the three St. Louis cemeteries. It tends not to be as crowded as the others, and while many of its inhabitants are not as well-known as those in St. Louis #1, there are several notables.

Ernest Bellocq, known for his photographs of Storyville prostitutes, is here, as is the noted architect James Gallier Sr. Margaret Haughery, who we discussed in the section about the Lower Garden District, is buried in St. Louis #3, as is Earnest "Dutch" Morial, the first black mayor of New Orleans. Of significance to me, my maternal grandparents are buried here.

St. Louis #3 is known as the "Cemetery of Angels" due to the large number of angels that decorate many of the tombs. This makes it a good cemetery for photographers.

New Orleans Fairgrounds (fairgroundsracecourse.com; 1751 Gentilly Blvd.; 504-944-5515) is the nation's third-oldest horse track and has been around since 1872. The season begins on Thanksgiving Day and continues into late March. Thanksgiving is a popular day, with families attending the races and enjoying a traditional lunch. After the horse racing season ends, the fairgrounds are home to the New Orleans Jazz & Heritage Festival, hosting hundreds of thousands of visitors and more than 100 musical acts over the last weekend in April and the first weekend in May.

The second option on the red streetcar is to skip the Carrollton extension and ride to the end of Canal Street. At that end, you'll find a plethora of cemeteries including Charity Hospital Cemetery, St. Patrick, Cypress Grove, Greenwood, Lakelawn, and Metairie. They range from the very small to quite large. Greenwood and Metairie are the largest and feature ornate tombs and mausoleums. Again, these are destinations for the photographer.

As you approach the end of the Canal line, there is a small **Hurricane Katrina Memorial** on your left. From above you can see it is shaped like the symbol used for hurricanes in weather forecasts. The memorial includes six small mausoleums containing the remains of those whose bodies were not claimed after the storm. It is a powerful reminder of the destruction and loss of life.

CITY PARK

City Park is 50 percent larger than New York's Central Park. It covers 1,300 acres and includes a golf course, the New Orleans Museum of Art, a walking and running path, a children's amusement park, and the Children's Museum, just to name a few. If you take the red streetcar to the end of the Carrollton extension, you'll reach City Park. The park

City Park peristyle and lagoon MARK BOLOGNA

will be on your left and Bayou St. John on your right.

If you took the streetcar to get here and are up for a bit of a walk, try this: Walk back about a block until you get to City Park Avenue, then turn right. You are now at the edge of the park. As you walk down the sidewalk or, better yet, weave through the trees, you are in the oldest grove of live oaks in City Park. Some of the oak trees here are nearly 800 years old.

These trees were often the site of duels in the 1800s and, sadly, the occasional suicide. Today they host much more cheerful proceedings. You'll often see kids climbing the branches, and it is a favorite spot for family photos or wedding portraits, as well as the occasional wedding. During the annual **Celebration in the Oaks** between Thanksgiving and New Year's, these trees are filled with millions of bright lights and surrounded by displays celebrating holiday traditions.

If you wander down a block or two, you'll notice a small concrete and stone pedestrian bridge that crosses over the lagoon. Cross that bridge if you are ready for a break, or keep exploring. I used to spend hours running around back here as a kid. In fact, there is another even smaller bridge farther down. We spent many hours running up and over that bridge. My mom, who is a wonderful artist, painted a scene from here for me many years ago. It hangs in our dining room and is one of my prized possessions.

OK, when you're finished here, go across that first bridge. You'll be directly behind a 1930s-era structure referred to locally as the Casino. Walk around to the left: you'll see a large playground area for the kids. On this side of the Casino, you'll also find **Cafe du Monde** (shop.cafedumonde.com; 56 Dreyfous Dr.; 504-766-0250), a beignet place that is a sister to the Cafe du Monde in the French Quarter. For obvious

City Park stone bridge **MARK BOLOGNA**

reasons, this is a favorite with my kids. If you haven't had beignets yet on this visit, stop now and enjoy!

This is also a great insider tip to keep in mind when visiting, especially if you have a car. As you'll see, there are lots of things to do here, you can always find parking, and it is nearly always less crowded than the Cafe du Monde down in the Quarter. For those reasons, it's become our go-to beignet stop. The kids ask to come here at least a couple of times a month. It has the added bonus of a large playground next door: perfect for burning off that sugar.

Another fun option for the younger ones is **Storyland** (neworleanscitypark.com/in-the-park/storyland; 5 Victory Ave.; 504-483-9402), a small amusement park. To get there from the playground area, cross the street and go through the parking lot. When you get to the other side, Storyland will be across the street and just to the left a bit. At $6 a person at the time of this writing, it's certainly affordable. The kids can explore nursery rhyme–themed displays, including the Three Little Pigs and Cinderella's carriage. In all, there are 26 exhibits, and the characters are sculptures created by New Orleans Mardi Gras float makers!

There are lots of places to sit, lots of shade, and my kids' favorite: the fire-breathing dragon slide. The steps go up its back while the slide itself goes down the fire! Inside the park there are rides and a beautiful enclosed carousel. Nearby are ticket windows where you can purchase tickets for the rides.

Behind the carousel is where you can purchase a ticket and board the **City Park Train** (neworleanscitypark.org/venues/train-ride; 7 Victory Ave.; 504-482-4888). This mini train is a fun way to take a tour of a portion of the park, including that old grove of live oaks we went through a few minutes ago. During Celebration in the Oaks, the train is very popular and a fun way to see the millions of lights strung throughout the trees.

If your kids are older, you might check out the minigolf course, aptly named **City Putt** (neworleanscitypark.com/in-the-park/city-putt; 33 Dreyfous Dr.; 504-483-9385). Located just outside Storyland, there are two courses: one has a New Orleans theme, while the other is focused on Louisiana as a whole.

City Park sculpture in fountain **MARK BOLOGNA**

As you walk back towards the front of the park and the Museum of Art, you'll come upon a sculpture garden. There are some sculptures sure to catch the attention of your kids no matter the age. My children like the LOVE (L-O-V-E) sculpture and the large daddy longlegs spider, though it's a love-hate relationship with that thing. You've seen similar images of the word *LOVE*: the one with the *O* turned sideways. One note: The workers here tend to get a little militant about photos for some reason, so if you want to take a picture of little Susie next to the LOVE sculpture, do it quickly when no one is looking!

Back towards the front, if you go around the Museum of Art headed towards the streetcar, you'll notice a lake to your left. There was always a lagoon here, but it was surrounded on three sides by part of an executive-style golf course. Post-Katrina, they removed the golf course and reshaped the lagoon into what is now called **Big Lake.** It is a replica of the other lake down the street a couple of miles: Lake

INSIDER TIP: That playground near the Casino is large and lots of fun, but frequently crowded. However, near Big Lake on the north side, there is a much smaller play spot. It is named the **Sir Cumference Playground** and is located near the Festival Grounds and Christian Brothers school. It is always less crowded than the other spot, and my kids love the unique attractions here including several climbing areas, a balance beam, and musical instruments. The City Park website states this playground is geared towards kids 5 to 12. Just be prepared, as you may need to climb up a rope structure to "rescue" a child if they get to the top and get a little spooked.

Pontchartrain! You can rent bikes here, including family bikes that hold four people. There are also pedal boats and rowboats. Lots to see and do here.

For adults, there is a botanical garden near Storyland. Additionally, the park was significantly updated in the 1930s under the Works Progress Administration. As a result, you'll find lots of small bridges, benches, and other features stamped with "W.P.A." One of my favorite features from that era are the Enrique Alvarez statues and reliefs on many of the concrete benches. You'll also find his work in both the botanical garden and the sculpture garden.

The **New Orleans Museum of Art** (noma.org; 1 Collins C. Diboll Circle; 504-658-4100) houses a permanent collection of 40,000 pieces with a large focus on French and American art, as well as a series of rotating and special exhibits.

For golf enthusiasts, City Park is home to two courses: a smaller, more recreational course and a PGA-style championship course for the more advanced golfer. There is also a double-decker driving range.

City Park Botanical Garden MARK BOLOGNA

In the middle of City Park is **Couturie Forest.** At 60 acres, it boasts the highest point of elevation in New Orleans, a whopping 43 feet above sea level. This small forest is a neat place for a peaceful walk and bird-watching in the center of the park.

City Park wildflowers **MARK BOLOGNA**

City Park is also home to the 20-court **City Park Tennis Center** (5900 Marconi Dr.; 504-483-9422) that offers hard and clay courts, as well as pickleball, a dog park (City Bark), numerous fountains and pavilions, and softball fields. **Tad Gormley Stadium** (5400 Stadium Dr.; 504-483-9363) is currently the site of a full schedule of high school football games each fall, but also hosted the 1992 US Olympic Track and Field Trials. Across the street the practice track created for the trials is open to the public.

Located in the heart of City Park, **Bayou Oaks at City Park** (cityparkgolf.com; 1040 Filmore Ave.; 504-483-9410) offers two 18-hole golf courses. The South Course was redesigned in 2017 and is the more challenging of the two. The North Course is the only one of the original four left more or less intact after Hurricane Katrina. It is a bit shorter and less challenging than the South Course, but is nonetheless fun for the mid-to-high handicapper (myself included!).

The **Festival Grounds** along Wisner Boulevard near Bayou St. John used to be the 18th fairway of a golf course before Hurricane Katrina. Today it hosts a calendar of festivals including the very popular Voodoo Fest, held on or near Halloween each year.

As you can see, there is no shortage of things to do and see in City Park. It's a must-stop if you are traveling with children, interested in photography, or just want to get out of the French Quarter and spend some time outdoors.

For even more information about City Park, listen to episode 33 of the *Beyond Bourbon Street* podcast.

Here's a list of my current top 10 things to do and see in City Park:

1. Old live oak grove
2. Beignets at Cafe du Monde
3. Storyland
4. Sculpture garden
5. City Putt
6. Botanical garden
7. Celebration in the Oaks
8. Couturie Forest
9. Concert or event at the Festival Grounds
10. New Orleans Museum of Art (NOMA)

GENTILLY

This largely residential neighborhood is located not far from Lake Pontchartrain, City Park, and Lakeview. You'll need a car or a rideshare or taxi to get to most places in Gentilly.

EAT

The Original Fiorella's Cafe (originalfiorellas.com; 5325 Franklin Ave.; 504-309-0352) is known for its award-winning fried chicken. They also make a range of excellent po-boys including fried shrimp, hot sausage, and roast beef. Daily plate lunch specials make this a favorite among locals.

Toast (toastneworleans.com; 1845 Gentilly Blvd.; 504-351-3664) is one of my favorite breakfast spots in the city. They are known for their aebelskivers—a Danish-inspired dish made of fried batter. At Toast, they are dusted with powdered sugar and served with your choice of dipping sauces. My favorites are the caramel and the lemon curd.

The Munch Factory (themunchfactory.net; 6514 Congress Dr.; 504-459-2180) is located in the clubhouse of the Joseph M. Bartholomew Municipal Golf Course, but don't let that keep you away. Their offerings punch way above what you'd expect. My favorite dishes are the chicken wings and the Munch Bowl—a portion of creamy, cheesy grits topped with house-made roast beef debris. *Note:* They also have a location at Louis Armstrong International Airport.

Zimmer's Seafood (4915 St. Anthony Ave.; 504-282-7150). This neighborhood seafood market offers po-boys at lunchtime, including one of the best fried shrimp po-boys around.

SEE & DO

Like much of New Orleans, Hurricane Katrina (2005) struck the Gentilly neighborhood with a vengeance. The London Avenue Canal suffered breaches to the levees on both sides, resulting in massive flooding of this neighborhood.

There is a small memorial titled the **Levee Exhibit Hall and Garden** (5000 Warrington Dr.). Not far from Zimmer's Seafood, this small outdoor exhibit is located at the site of one of the levee breaks and tells the story of what happened there.

THE LAKEFRONT, WEST END & BUCKTOWN

The lakefront of Lake Ponchartrain extends from the Seabrook Bridge to the Orleans Parish–Jefferson Parish line. The lakefront is a nice place for a picnic, a bike ride, or a run or walk along the levee that follows the road. In some places, neighborhoods abut the levee and offer a series of paths in a parklike setting. The lakefront seawall is also a popular place for locals to fish and crab, and to enjoy sunsets.

The West End used to be teeming with restaurants before Katrina. Most are gone, but there are still a few gems there.

Bucktown lies just across the parish border with Jefferson. This former fishing village has a couple good spots for local dining.

EAT

Russell's Marina Grill (russellsmarinagrill.net; 58555 Pontchartrain Blvd.; 504-282-9980) is open for breakfast and lunch. It's been around for decades and serves all the usual breakfast items, plus specials. Desserts are homemade. We visit Russell's a couple of times a year, and I'm always surprised by how much better it is than I expected. Portions are large here and the locals know it. It gets crowded, so expect a wait on weekends.

The Blue Crab (thebluecrabnola.com; 7900 Lakeshore Dr.; 504-284-2898) is a bit of a throwback to the type of restaurant found in this area prior to Hurricane Katrina. Focused on seafood and offering views of the lake and marina, it's especially nice when the weather is just a bit cooler.

Felix's (felixs.com; 7400 Lakeshore Dr.; 504-304-4125) is the sister to the same restaurant in the French Quarter. Known for raw oysters, they also offer the usual assortment of seafood dishes and platters, overlooking the marina.

Station 6 (station6nola.com; 105 Metairie Hammond Hwy.; 504-345-2936). Slightly upscale but still casual, this seafood restaurant offers dishes such as charbroiled redfish and seared pompano. Also has a raw oyster bar.

Deanie's Seafood (deanies.com; 1713 Lake St.; 504-831-4141) offers boiled seafood in season, raw oysters, po-boys, seafood platters, and more. One of the oldest seafood restaurants of its kind in New Orleans, it's popular with locals.

R&O's (216 Metairie Hammond Hwy.; 504-831-1248). Yet another neighborhood restaurant, this one offers an excellent seafood gumbo, a delicious shrimp po-boy, and one of the best roast beef po-boys in town.

SEE & DO

The allure of the lakefront is the view. In days past, there were amusement parks on the lakefront, but today it is mostly a haven for fishermen, sailors, runners, bicyclists, and those enjoying a picnic lunch.

The Mardi Gras Fountain pays tribute to the Mardi Gras organizations past and present. Each one is represented by a small plaque, emblazoned with the krewe's logo and colors.

The New Canal Lighthouse (8001 Lakeshore Dr.; 504-282-2134) was established in 1839. Guided tours are available.

Mardi Gras 2020: after Gras JAMES CULLEN

CELEBRATIONS

MARDI GRAS

You may be thinking of visiting New Orleans during Mardi Gras, or you may be scared to death of that idea. In this section, we'll break it all down for you, starting with this: Carnival and Mardi Gras are not the same thing.

Carnival season begins on Twelfth Night at the conclusion of the twelve days of Christmas, on January 6. That day is also known as the Feast of the Epiphany and as Kings Day. My kids refer to it as king cake day, but we'll get to that in a bit.

In Christian traditions it marks the day the Magi, or Three Wise Men, visited the Christ child, the baby Jesus. This also becomes important later on in our story.

Twelfth Night is the traditional end of the holiday season in the Christian world. I suppose in most places it means the start of the New Year, a time for resolutions, losing weight, etc., but not here in New Orleans. Instead, the party simply transitions from the festivities of the holiday season to Carnival.

One last note about the date. If anyone is reading in England, you are probably saying Twelfth Night is January 5. Here in New Orleans, it is celebrated on January 6, the 12th day after Christmas. I understand some religions and cultures count from Christmas Eve and celebrate Twelfth Night on January 5. Nonetheless, it is important to us in New Orleans because it is the start of Carnival season, which begins on January 6 and concludes at midnight on Mardi Gras (Fat Tuesday).

While the date of Mardi Gras varies, Twelfth Night does not. As a result, sometimes you have a long Carnival season and in other years you have a sprint.

In order to make your experience the best possible, it's a good idea to spend a little time planning. Mardi Gras truly has something for everyone. When I hear of people having a poor experience, it is usually because they didn't match their actions with their expectations. In this section, we are going to help you do just that.

Let's start with an inventory of you. Here are some questions to help:

- Who are you and what do you like?
- Are you the party animal, or are you the quiet observer at a cocktail party, taking it all in with an amused smile on your face?
- Are you more likely to paint your face at a football game or enjoy the view from a skybox?

WHERE DO YOU FALL ON THE PUBLIC NUDITY METER?

0: Ugh, no! I have kids and that's the last thing I need to see.

50: I'm indifferent. I'm not going to freak out if I see some nakedness, but I don't care one way or the other.

75: Sure, why not? I mean, I'm in New Orleans for Mardi Gras.

100: Definitely. Heck, I might even wear body paint as my costume!

- Who are you traveling with? Your spouse or partner? Kids? A large group?
- What about crowds? Are you comfortable being part of a sea of humanity, or do you prefer a little room to spread out?
- Do you drink alcohol?
- What is your reaction to the idea of costumes? Do you like to dress up, or does that make you roll your eyes? Are you interested, but prefer to observe rather than take part?
- When are you visiting?
- What is your budget?

Some additional questions to ask are: Do you know anyone who lives here? Will they be in town? Many schools in New Orleans are closed during the week of Mardi Gras. As a result, a lot of families choose to go on vacation that week and avoid the madness. Others split the difference and leave on Wednesday.

Will you have a car? More specifically, will you be driving to get to New Orleans or will you fly? My opinion is, if you don't need a car to get here, don't rent one.

WHERE TO STAY

I suggest you go back to the questions earlier in the chapter. Your expectations, budget, and who you are traveling with will help determine what will be the best fit for you.

If you want to spend most of your time in the French Quarter, look for a hotel in the Quarter or in the Central Business District or Warehouse District. You'll find plenty of options from boutique hotels to large national brands. The Sheraton on Canal Street is a nice blend in that it is on the edge of the Quarter but also has stands for viewing the parades that pass along Canal Street.

In the heart of the French Quarter are places like the Bourbon Orleans, the Royal Orleans, and the Prince Conti. A sneaky play is the Best Western in the Quarter. It tends to host the party crowd, but it

INSIDER TIP: **Plan early or very, very late. Most of the hotels in prime locations will be mostly booked a year out. They may require minimum stays, especially once you get to the Friday before Mardi Gras day. They do tend to release rooms, but you're taking a chance. Don't do that unless you are adventurous, not dead set on being here, or don't have kids.**

is nicer than you might expect for a Best Western, and if you are looking to be in the French Quarter for Mardi Gras, you are probably on the party end of the equation anyway.

In general, I recommend the area from Canal Street to Lee Circle, encompassing the border between the French Quarter and the Central Business District, and continuing into the Warehouse District. Just past Lee Circle you reach the Garden District, which does not have many hotel options.

A little farther Uptown are a couple of nice options right on St. Charles, but the Central Business District and Warehouse District give you a nice blend. You can head to the French Quarter if you want, or have a wealth of parade viewing options. It's tough to recommend specific hotels, because so much depends on your budget and how early you plan.

If I had to recommend one hotel, almost regardless of your situation, it would the Renaissance Arts in the Warehouse District on Tchoupitoulas Street. I like this hotel because it is in a great location and is just the right size. Most of the parades pass within a few blocks of the hotel, and two of the biggest, Bacchus and Orpheus, parade right in front.

The Renaissance is an easy walk to the French Quarter, and you have a host of great dining options nearby. Additionally, I like the size of the hotel. It is only four floors tall, so if you want to run back in—say, to go to the bathroom, grab a snack or a beer from your room, or just take a break—you don't have to wait for the elevators. Sometimes in the big hotels, this can be a problem. Something to think about. In any event, keep this hotel in mind, not just for Carnival but for any visit to New Orleans.

A longtime sponsor of the *Beyond Bourbon Street* podcast is the Old No. 77 Hotel and Chandlery. It is located just down the street from the Renaissance and is my favorite hotel in general, but especially for Mardi Gras, if you don't want/need to stay in a place where you can use hotel points.

The one downside to staying in the Central Business or Warehouse District is that you are farther down the parade route. This means the parades arrive at your location sometimes hours after they start. This can make for a very long day and is something to consider, especially with young kids.

Mardi Gras parade ladders **MARK BOLOGNA**

One other point: Stay somewhere on or very close to the parade route. And stay in New Orleans. Every year, I see people ask online about staying in Metairie or Kenner, suburbs of New Orleans. You could do that, but you will be encountering transportation problems and, in my opinion, lose out on the best of Carnival: that is, immersing yourself in the community.

Plus, the days can be long. Why compete with thousands of others looking for a taxi or a rideshare? You certainly don't want to be driving if you've been enjoying an adult beverage or two. Even if you have not, you can be assured many people have. It's just not the best time to be driving.

Mardi Gras is about being a part of the community. You'll want to get out on the route early, with plenty of time to settle in and meet your neighbors. You might also want to linger afterwards, or wander off just before the last couple of floats appear and duck in someplace for a meal. You won't do those things if you're worried about commuting back to a hotel outside the city.

One caveat to this recommendation: If you are staying with friends who live in New Orleans and know the place, then by all means stay with them if they'll have you. Even if they live in the suburbs, they will know their way around. Plus, they'll probably drive, so you won't have to.

WHAT TO WEAR

Let's talk clothing. Dress appropriately.

First up, shoes. I cannot overstate this one. Ladies, please don't wear high heels. Flip-flops are not the best idea either. Wear comfortable shoes that you don't mind getting dirty. It can be a long day and the streets can get pretty gross, especially if it has been raining.

My wife has "Mardi Gras" tennis shoes. They are an old pair of black running shoes. Perfect. Comfortable and they hide dirt. She hoses them out when we get home.

Willie Wonka and friends MARK BOLOGNA

There's another reason footwear is important: doubloons. Though they have diminished in popularity, doubloons are basically large coins thrown in some parades. They are usually anodized aluminum and come in a variety of colors, though the best known is the gold one thrown by members of the Rex parade. Rex was the first krewe to throw doubloons when they started the practice in 1960.

On one side of the doubloon is the insignia of the Carnival krewe. On the other is the theme of the parade for that year. Often when doubloons are tossed, they end up hitting the ground. Do *not* try to pick one up. Rather, you step on it with your foot, then calmly lean over, move your foot, and pick it up. If you are wearing flip-flops, you will get your foot smashed. If you are wearing heels, you'll get knocked over or break your heel.

Next, wear layers. I can't tell you how many times I've been at a parade and ended up standing next to someone from out of town. The conversation goes something like this:

Me:	Where you from?
Visitor:	Ohio [or New York, or Michigan, or Minnesota].
Me:	Having a good time?
Visitor:	Yeah, but it is a lot colder than we thought. Where we live 50 isn't bad, but we are freezing out here!

The thing people underestimate is the dampness. We're in a swamp. It's wet. Not the ground, the air. I lived in Minnesota for two years: the difference is the humidity. Fifty degrees here is chilly. Forty and below is bone chilling, especially when you are standing outside for hours. When I lived in Minnesota, it felt like 30 to 35 degrees was balmy. After you got used to it, you could go outside in shirtsleeves. You don't want to do that at Mardi Gras. You'll be miserable.

Wear a hat. It's often sunny, no matter the temperature. You'll get sunburned before you know it. You know what is not fun? That moment you put a string of beads around your neck only to feel the sting when you rub those beads across your crispy skin.

One of the hazards of Mardi Gras are flying beads. They hurt when they hit, especially if they hit your face. It happens all the time.

Speaking from experience, when you ride on a float, you are excited. You may also be intoxicated. You see a cute kid, a friendly face, an attractive woman or man. You make eye contact and decide to throw them some beads. It can be a fair distance, and you are on a moving float. It takes some effort. If you judge any of those variables incorrectly, you can end up smacking someone across the face. Additionally, some people are just jerks. It's part of life. Some of those people end up snockered and on Mardi Gras floats. They fling beads indiscriminately and think they are being cute. They aren't.

If you wear a hat, particularly a baseball cap, it can help minimize the risk of getting hit in the face because the bill may deflect the beads. This is a particular hazard for small kids sitting on their

INSIDER TIP: If you use sunscreen on your neck, don't put beads around your neck. The sunscreen does something to the colors, and you will end up staining both your neck and your clothes. Another option is to wear a dark shirt. This will also help hide all the spills and dirt.

dad's shoulders or in a parade ladder. Every year I think about developing the Mardi Gras shield. It would have a purple, green, and gold hardhat component with a ventilated plastic shield that flips down. If you take this idea and bring it to market, I want one.

Let's recap clothing before we move on. Wear comfortable shoes that can get dirty. Dress in layers. Wear a hat and also sunglasses during the day. It is also useful to wear pants with a decent amount of pockets, as opposed to skintight jeans.

MARDI GRAS TOOLKIT

The first rule of Mardi Gras is to travel as light as you can and be self-sustaining. Here's what you need:

- Lightweight backpack
- *Arthur Hardy's Mardi Gras Guide*. You'll get the route maps, start times, and some history of the individual krewes.
- Parade tracking app from local TV stations WWL and WDSU. Parades do have a start time, but there are often delays: floats break down, people get hurt, etc.
- Snacks
- Water
- Battery backup and cable for your phone
- Toilet paper
- Wet wipes
- Sanitizing hand gel
- Plastic bags
- Something to put throws into, especially with kids. You will catch a lot, and the kids will want to keep them. This is especially true on Mardi Gras day.
- Sunscreen
- Can koozies—collapsible so they fit in your back pocket

Optional:

- Bag chairs
- Ice chest
- Drinks
- Food
- Parade ladder

The key is to bring the essentials and little else. Having said that, let's talk about the parade ladder for a minute. This is an essential for any New Orleans family with kids. Basically, it's a 6-foot stepladder with a wooden box on top. The box is usually homemade, though you can buy them at a couple of the small, neighborhood hardware stores. The box has a back and sides, but no front. Across the front is a dowel, made out of wood or PVC pipe. The dowel slides through holes in each side and is secured in place with a bolt or a pin.

You put the kids in the box, and an adult stands behind them to anchor the whole thing and to help catch throws for them. It serves several purposes: the kids can see the parade, you don't have to worry about them running out in the street, and they are attractive targets for the masked float riders.

Mardi Gras parade ladders **MARK BOLOGNA**

I know this must sound crazy, but trust me, anyone who grew up here has fond memories of their parade ladder. It's a New Orleans tradition. If you are out on the route and someone offers to let your child get in the ladder, take them up on it. You'll see them all over the parade route as well.

Note: Parade ladders need to be set up at least 6 feet from the curb and should not be chained to each other.

SAFETY

No doubt, you've heard stories about how bad the crime is in New Orleans. On the one hand, some of it is true. The police force is understaffed here. On the other hand, this is a big city. And like all big cities, we do have our share of crime. For the most part, if you use common sense, stay with the crowds, and avoid poorly lit places off the beaten path, you should be fine.

Here are some tips to follow:

Leave the jewelry at home or at the very least locked in the safe in your room. You don't want to make yourself an easy target by displaying flashy jewelry. Also, rings and watches can easily get tangled up with Mardi Gras beads.

I've seen people lose rings or have the prongs on an engagement ring get damaged. I've had more than one watch pulled off my arm when a pair of beads got wrapped around the watch face. The other thing that can happen is your ring can go flying off as you wave your hands in the air, especially if the weather is cool or if you've been eating fried chicken and have greasy fingers.

Put your money, credit cards, etc., in your front pants pocket. Even better is to wrap a rubber band around them to make it a little more difficult to pull those items out.

If you decide to wander onto Bourbon Street to take in the craziness there, you will undoubtedly see throngs of people looking up at the balconies, arms outstretched begging for beads. When the crowd gets really worked up, the pickpockets swarm in. A friend of ours who is a policeman actually showed us this one year from a balcony. Sure enough, a woman lifted her shirt at the urging of someone on a balcony, the crowd went nuts, and three or four people immediately went into the fray, lifting wallets. Keep in mind, sometimes these folks work in groups. One person causes a scene to create a distraction so the others can prey upon unsuspecting people in the crowd.

A different type of safety tip has to do with interacting with the parades themselves. The floats are pulled by tractors in most cases. In 2020, two people got run over and were killed. Invariably someone gets too close to the side of a float or is looking ahead and runs right in front of one. Particularly tragic are cases where a child runs after something thrown and ends up under a float. These things are easily

Mardi Gras marching bands JAMES CULLEN

preventable by watching out for your party and for others around you. In general, the crowd is good about this and about taking care of others, but you do want to be mindful, especially at the big parades. The crowds can get really thick and sometimes are very close to the floats.

I'm certainly not trying to scare you. Given the number of people, everything that is going on, and all the distractions, Mardi Gras is still a very safe, fun event. A little precaution and awareness can help ensure you have a great time.

PARKING

My advice is don't have a car if you can avoid it. However, if you drive into town or for whatever reason decide to rent a vehicle, here are some tips.

The first option is to pay for parking along the parade route. Some schools and churches along or near the route offer parking, usually by reservation, and the price varies by day—more expensive for the biggest parades and Mardi Gras day.

Mardi Gras: No Parking **MARK BOLOGNA**

Sacred Heart on the corner of Napoleon and St. Charles is a great spot. Just down St. Charles towards Downtown is New Orleans Hamburger & Seafood. They usually offer a package deal of parking and inside access, which means bathrooms, etc. On the other side of St. Charles (the river side) about two blocks away from the direction the parades travel, there is St. George's Episcopal Church. While they don't have parking, in most years they offer free bathrooms and sell food. In fact, many churches along the route do this, so keep your eye out.

You can also park your car ahead of time. This requires planning and some effort. Park the car in a good spot, then leave it. Go for a walk, run, take the streetcar. Obtain transportation back to the route for the parade, then pick up your car afterwards. This is also useful if you have kids and/or a ton of stuff.

We actually do a variation on this theme for the big parades and for Mardi Gras day. I go out early or even the night before, leave my car in the best spot I can find, then head home. Sometimes I run, other times I take the streetcar. When it is time to go to the parade, we pile into the minivan and drive back to my car. If we find a good spot, we park. If not, I hop out and move my car, while my wife pulls in with the minivan. I drive my car to the best spot I can find, usually just a few blocks away, then walk back. It may seem like a lot, but it ensures us of a good spot for the van. This is important when we're going to be out on the route for a while, or if the weather is not great—especially with young kids.

Here's another option if you've driven into town: Years ago, before my wife and I moved back, we would come home for Mardi Gras. One year we stayed at the Sheraton on Canal—a good central spot, by the way. After I dropped Marie off with our stuff, I drove the car into the Garden District, found a quiet street, and left it. I think I ran back to the hotel, though I might've taken a streetcar. We left the car there for a couple days, then I went back and retrieved it. *Note:* Some streets and areas are marked residential. If you leave a car like this, you run the risk of a parking ticket, though it will almost certainly be cheaper than parking at a hotel.

One final option: Park away from the route and walk. This is fun if you are traveling light and without children. I like to park on St. Charles, on the Uptown side of Napoleon—basically on St. Charles in the opposite direction from where the parades are heading. You'll understand this when you see it. Others park much farther down and take the streetcar back.

Again, my best tip on this is to avoid driving if you can. Before we had kids and were living out of town, we would come home for Mardi Gras, as I mentioned a moment ago. Some of our best experiences were staying Downtown and walking the length of the route with only a backpack. We would stop to watch the parade or grab a beer. Invariably, we would see friends along the way. If we made it to the beginning of the parade, we would meet up with my parents, and maybe get a ride back. If not, we knew the worst-case scenario was a long but leisurely walk back to the hotel.

This is a colorful and fun way to experience Mardi Gras. You get to see the various ways people are celebrating, the costumes, just the feel of the experience. It's still one of my favorite ways to do it, and every chance we get, we take the kids for a leisurely walk down the route.

OK, one last general item I think we need to cover . . .

WHERE TO GO TO THE BATHROOM

This is a big deal. Don't underestimate this one. You're out on the parade route for hours. You might be enjoying a beer or two. If you have kids, they'll certainly need to go at some point.

New Orleans is a pretty tolerant town—but the easiest way to get arrested in New Orleans during Carnival is to pee in public. It's where we draw the line. Many of us have done it at some point, but if you get caught you're probably getting arrested for indecent exposure. Additionally, you won't find yourself getting processed and released quickly, especially over the weekend right before Mardi Gras. You could be in an Orleans Parish jail for longer than expected, which is not the experience you were hoping for.

There is some good news, though. With just a little planning, you'll be fine. Again, the corner of St. Charles and Napoleon is where you'll find Sacred Heart Academy. As a fund-raiser, the men's club at the school sells wristbands allowing access to their porta-potties, which they clean after each use. Some of the churches along the route will even allow you to go in and use the facilities for free, though it changes from year to year in terms of which are open.

Another option is a restaurant or bar. Most require that you make a purchase, and the lines can sometimes be long, but it is an option, especially if you are standing right outside a place to watch the parade.

The city also provides port-a-potties along the route. These are fine, though they don't get cleaned often and lines will form, especially at the larger parades. This is also where the tip about packing your own toilet paper comes in handy.

Truthfully, the only time I've run into a problem finding a bathroom has been at the most popular parades, and mostly on Saturday and Sunday nights before Mardi Gras. On those nights, two of the largest parades, known as superkrewes, hold their processions. Endymion is first on Saturday evening, with Bacchus holding the Sunday night slot. These parades attract enormous crowds who spend the day, and sometimes even a couple of nights before, camped out to secure their spot. It is not unusual to have places along the route where the crowd is 20 to 30 people deep. As you can imagine, the lines to use the limited porta-potties can get quite long.

THE PARADES

Carnival season begins on Twelfth Night and ends at midnight on Mardi Gras. After the couple of parades on Twelfth Night, things calm down parade-wise until two weekends before Mardi Gras. Most locals refer to the weekend when parades get into gear as the first weekend of parade season. This is a fun time. The parades are not the largest or most extravagant, but the crowds are reasonable and you get a good taste of Carnival. It's a great weekend for families because you will have room to spread out and let the kids run a bit.

Typically, there are five parades on Saturday and another four on Sunday. You won't see many costumes among the crowd, so if that's

Mardi Gras: Bacca-Whoppa **JAMES CULLEN**

your thing, you want to be here on Mardi Gras. This first weekend is a good intro to Carnival and certainly a good time with the kids. This weekend in many ways has become my favorite part of Carnival. It's not the weekend to visit if you want to take part in the madness in the French Quarter, but it is a great option for everyone else.

Things pick up again on the Wednesday and Thursday before Mardi Gras. These days have really amped up in recent years. Each of these nights has a top-notch parade and sometimes two. The crowds will be large and enthusiastic but navigable.

On Wednesday, things kick off with the Mystic Krewe of Druids. Druids traces its lineage back to an earlier parade of the same name and uses some of the original float carriages from nearly 100 years ago.

Thursday evening brings a trifecta of parades along the traditional Uptown route. Leading off the evening are the Knights of Babylon. Founded in 1939, they adhere to the traditions of the older krewes. Of note, their king's float is pulled by a mule, instead of the tractors used by most modern parades. The king is accompanied by flambeaux to light his path.

The Knights of Chaos follow Babylon. This night of Carnival used to be known as Momus Thursday and was the domain of the Knights of Momus from 1872 until 1991, when they ceased parading in protest of a city council ordinance that required Carnival organizations to disclose their membership. In its place the Krewe of Chaos was formed in 2000. They purchased the Momus floats and continue the Momus tradition of satirical themes.

Next up is the all-female Krewe of Muses. Muses was formed in 2000 and quickly became a hit. Their signature throw is the hand-decorated shoe, which is perhaps the catch to have after the Zulu coconut. Muses is named after the nine daughters of Zeus, but has a New Orleans connection. Several streets in the Lower Garden District are named after the Muses. Here's some insider knowledge: three of them are traditionally mispronounced by locals—Calliope, Terpsichore, and Melpomene (CAL-e-o, TERP-si-core, MEL-po-mean).

This night gets large crowds but is great fun. You could arrive in New Orleans Wednesday morning and leave Sunday or Monday and have a wonderful experience.

Thursday is also when you will start to see the crowds build in the French Quarter. You'll be able to move around and might even be able to score a perch on a balcony, but tonight's the night if you want that experience and don't want to be in a mass of people.

Next up is the weekend before Mardi Gras. This is go time. Friday is when the French Quarter will close to vehicular traffic. It's the last day I enjoy walking in the Quarter until Mardi Gras morning.

On Friday evening you have a bundle of parades, starting with the Krewe of Hermes. Founded in 1937, Hermes is the Carnival organization with the longest record of hosting a nighttime parade in New Orleans. They traditionally make great use of lighting, and were the first organization to use neon lights on their floats, in 1938. Today, even the riders' costumes are lighted. They also have great bands each year.

Hermes is followed by one of my favorites, Le Krewe d'Etat. They were formed in 1996 and had from their beginnings the intention of reaching back to the satirical themes favored by some of the early organizations like Momus.

The Krewe of Morpheus rounds out this trio of parades on Friday evening. Morpheus is a fun parade and is one of the few that are coed, whereas most krewes are all male or all female.

Mardi Gras Skull and Bones Gang JAMES CULLEN

Before we move on, a note about the Uptown New Orleans parade route. Post-Katrina, there has been a move to consolidate parades onto what is known as the traditional Uptown route. This was done largely as a measure to make it easier for a strapped police department to manage: having multiple routes across the city was getting more difficult to handle effectively.

The negative effect is the loss of neighborhood parades. Additionally, moving the parades onto one route has added more people onto those paths. Personally, I also think some of those parades were fine as a neighborhood parade, but don't quite live up to the splendor of the larger parades that traditionally dominated the Uptown route.

The reality is any parade is as fun as you make it. I mean, in most other places in the world people are cooking dinner, working, or doing normal, everyday things. We are putting the kids in parade ladders, grabbing an ice chest of beer, and heading out to enjoy a few hours of partying with new and old friends alike.

The benefit of this offshoot is particularly notable on the Friday evening: several parades have moved physically farther back, extending the start of the traditional route back along Magazine Street towards Audubon Park. This has been a fabulous development. While Magazine is narrow, it is lined with shops, restaurants, and bars. It is also in a neighborhood and so brings some of that feel to it. Magazine Street from the start at Jefferson is a terrific place to see the parades and is full of families enjoying themselves and each other. Even if you don't have kids, I would encourage you to catch a parade on Magazine Street, anywhere between Jefferson and Napoleon Avenue.

On Saturday, you have more choices. If I were visiting and did not have kids, I would make Endymion the focus. It is a spectacle in every way: the crowds, the size and extravagance of the parade. It violates my earlier mention about the loss of neighborhood routes as well. Endymion starts in Midcity, on the edge of City Park near Delgado Community College. Orleans Avenue, which is the first leg, is a sea of humanity. Controversially, people start trying to reserve space on the neutral ground a week before. By Wednesday or Thursday evening, you'll see people actually camping out to get a good spot.

The houses along the route take great pride in celebrating Endymion. Many create custom banners welcoming the krewe. There is also a stage on the neutral ground hosting music throughout the day. Another feature in recent years is that the riders walk down Orleans Avenue before boarding their floats for the ride. When I was in my 20s, I helped cohost a party for 1,000 or more people each year, complete with porta-potties, many kegs of beer, and a raised viewing platform. We would be out on the neutral ground by 7 a.m. and not leave until 11 or 12 at night. Those days are long gone, but it was a lot of fun.

Endymion is a superkrewe. There is no formal definition, but these are the largest organizations. Endymion has 3,100 all-male krewe members. They continually create larger and larger floats: the largest at present is a nine-section celebration of Pontchartrain Beach, a now-defunct amusement park in New Orleans. This float alone holds 250 riders, while some organizations have 500 in an entire parade.

Endymion has a celebrity serving as grand marshal each year. It is also one of only a few krewes that end their ride with a ball of sorts open to the public. Endymion parades right into the Superdome, where they disembark and join thousands of guests who are dressed in formal wear. Music on multiple stages goes on until the early hours of Sunday morning.

During the earlier part of Saturday, you can take in the all-female Krewe of Iris and the irreverent Krewe of Tucks, whose monarch sits upon an oversized toilet as a throne. Throws include decorated plungers, mini potties, and purple, green, and gold toilet paper.

Sunday is known as Thoth Sunday. It is a large, wonderfully colorful daytime parade with a solid mission at heart. Besides entertaining the general population, they start their route at Children's Hospital. For many families, this is Mardi Gras. They watch the parade, host or attend a large after-party, then head off on vacation the next day to escape the craziness.

Sunday evening is Bacchus, named after the god of wine. Bacchus was founded in 1968 and was the first superkrewe, introducing the idea of a celebrity grand marshal and a party open to anyone willing to pay an admission fee and dress up in their finest evening wear.

Monday is a day of recovery, but also a great time to visit the French Quarter. Known as Lundi Gras, you can find a festival taking place along the riverfront at Woldenberg Park. You can take in great local music, enjoy New Orleans food, and witness the arrival of Zulu and his queen by boat.

That night offers two parades, a perfect mix of new and old. The Krewe of Proteus leads off. Founded in 1882, they are one of the oldest parades. The king's float has a distinctive seashell and is accompanied by flambeaux, the flaming torches used in the 1800s to light the way.

Compared to Proteus is Orpheus, a mere child in comparison. Orpheus was founded in 1994 by local Harry Connick Jr. Appropriately enough, the name was chosen to honor the god of music and is a tribute to Harry's musical roots. Orpheus was formed to replace Proteus, which did not parade from 1993 to 1999 in protest of the 1992 city ordinance requiring Carnival organizations to disclose their

Bacchasaurus **JAMES CULLEN**

membership. Nonetheless, Lundi Gras is now as good as ever, with both the new and the old parading through Uptown New Orleans.

Last, but not least, is Mardi Gras: Fat Tuesday. The final day of Carnival starts with the processions of Zulu and Rex, followed by truck parades. These are made up of floats built on top of flatbed eighteen-wheelers.

Mardi Gras: Zulu Warriors **JAMES CULLEN**

Each truck is really a Carnival organization unto itself, mostly composed of families. You'll see men, women, and kids of all ages on these floats, taking part in the tradition of riding and offering throws to the crowd. Mardi Gras is also the day for families, with lots of costumes and an abundance of throws to beg for and catch. It really is one big party, and much more family oriented than television reports would have you believe. In fact, it is rare to see anything too racy outside the French Quarter.

If racy is what you want, head into the Quarter early and be sure to catch the drag queen costume contest: absolutely incredible, over-the-top costumes. If wild and crazy Mardi Gras is what you've come to New Orleans to experience, this is where it's at.

Enjoy the show, wander up to Canal Street to see Zulu and Rex, then join the flood of people on Bourbon Street celebrating the final hours of Carnival. The day and Carnival end with the meeting of the courts of two of the oldest Carnival organizations: Comus and Rex. At midnight, the chief of police and the mayor of the city of New Orleans ride down Bourbon Street on horseback, announcing the end of Carnival and the beginning of Lent.

Mardi Gras: Rex, King of Carnival **MARK BOLOGNA**

Mardi Gras, and New Orleans in general, is so much more than Bourbon Street debauchery. Sure, that can be part of your experience, but for the most part that is contained in the French Quarter.

Instead, when I think of the Mardi Gras I grew up with, and the one my kids are living today, it is filled with memories of days spent on the neutral ground of St. Charles Avenue and the sidewalks of Magazine

Street, of kids playing catch in the street while parents sip a beer and catch up with new and old friends.

It is enjoying the celebration New Orleans throws for itself each year. The *Beyond Bourbon Street* podcast was created because I got sick of hearing the narrative portrayed in the national media each year—that of boobs and drunkenness. Yes, you can have that, but it's a small part of Mardi Gras. My goal here and on the podcast is to provide you with the insight that comes from living and experiencing New Orleans as a local.

MARDI GRAS VOCABULARY

Now for a few words about the language of Mardi Gras. New Orleans has its own language. Words we use here aren't particularly common in other parts of the country, which is something we discussed earlier. This is true of Mardi Gras as well.

Neutral ground or sidewalk side? You'll hear this frequently. In fact, my kids don't think of the car as driver's side or passenger's side. They will tell you who sits on the neutral ground side (Olivia) and who has the sidewalk side (Sophia). Neutral ground refers to the grassy strip separating lanes of traffic. You might know it as the median. It is also where the streetcars run on St. Charles Avenue.

Krewe is the term used to refer to a carnival organization, as in the Krewe of Muses.

Captain: While many crews have a king, the captain of a parade is the leader, the chief operating officer if you will. He is in control.

Doubloons: We mentioned these earlier. First coined in 1960 by Rex, they are metal or wooden coins thrown or handed out. They have faded in popularity, but are still offered in many parades.

Flambeaux refer to the torches carried in some parades. This was the original method of lighting the path for the Mistick Krewe of Comus when they created the modern Carnival traditions of New Orleans in 1857.

Lundi Gras is Fat Monday, the day before Mardi Gras. Traditionally, this is the day Rex, King of Carnival, would make his formal entrance into the city by riverboat on the Mississippi. In recent years, the traditions have varied. Sometimes, Rex and Zulu arrive at the same time and meet for a toast and a proclamation from the mayor of New Orleans.

FESTIVALS & EVENTS

Festivals are a big part of life in New Orleans. They dot the calendar throughout the year, but really pick up in March and continue in earnest through October. They range from small, neighborhood events to among the largest in the country.

My advice? Plan your visit around the biggest events (Jazz Fest, Essence Fest, French Quarter Festival, Voodoo Fest) if those interest you and you've been to New Orleans before. Otherwise, visit when the time and weather fit you best, then look to see what festivals might be going on during your stay.

The number of events and dates change each year. Some festivals, like Jazz Fest, are locked into certain dates, but others vary a bit. Some change due to weather, and new ones appear all the time. I've listed some of my favorites below along with the month they usually happen. NewOrleans.com has a comprehensive list with a description of each festival, prices, and links to websites (neworleans.com/things-to-do/festivals). Be sure to check it before you make travel plans.

JANUARY

King Cake Festival: Usually held at Champions Square next to the Superdome. Several dozen vendors offer a wide variety of king cakes. There's also live music, a kids' area, and a king cake contest (kingcakefestival.org).

FEBRUARY

Tet Fest: Celebrates the Vietnamese New Year.

Lundi Gras (Zulu Lundi Gras Festival): Date varies based on Mardi Gras, but this event is held on Lundi Gras, the day before Fat Tuesday. It includes music, food, and the arrival of Zulu and Rex via the Mississippi River (lundigrasfestival.com).

MARCH

Mardi Gras Indians Super Sunday: On the Sunday nearest St. Joseph's Day, Mardi Gras Indians parade along the same route. This is different than Mardi Gras morning, when they each take their own route. Super

Sunday is not really a festival but is one of the most unique events in the city.

Wednesday at the Square Concert Series: Held in Lafayette Square in the Central Business District, this after-work hours weekly event from March to May is very popular among locals. Free live music along with local food vendors and artists (ylcnola.org/ylc-wednesday-at-the-square).

New Orleans Bourbon Festival: This festival includes learning sessions and talks with bourbon experts as well as a grand tasting event. If you love bourbon, this is one worth planning your trip around (neworleansbourbonfestival.com).

New Orleans Entrepreneur Week (NOEW): New Orleans did not have a big technology sector prior to Katrina, but it improves each year. NOEW is a chance to learn about new start-ups and includes, among other things, a start-up contest focused on companies that have ideas for tackling climate change and coastal erosion (noew.org).

Tennessee Williams Literary Festival: Typically held close to Williams's birthday, March 26, this five-day festival includes writers workshops, performances, book sales, and more (tennesseewilliams.net).

Hogs for the Cause: BBQ cook-off where dozens of teams vie for awards and sell their dishes to raise money for various charitable organizations. This popular event includes live music and delicious BBQ (hogsforthecause.org).

Congo Square New World Rhythms Festival: Celebration of the music and dance traditions of Africa, with live music, an arts market, and soul food (events.jazzandheritage.org).

APRIL

New Orleans Wine and Food Experience: Wine and food tastings, chef competitions, and more (nowfe.com).

Freret Street Festival: Live music, food, and crafts occupying several blocks of Freret Street (freretstreetfestival.org).

French Quarter Festival: One of the largest festivals of the year. As the name implies, this music festival takes place at multiple venues throughout the French Quarter. Unlike Jazz Fest, attendance at all of the stages is free; all you have to purchase are food and drink as you wander the French Quarter. The festival has many of the same performers as Jazz Fest, but focuses almost exclusively on musicians from New Orleans and to a lesser extent Louisiana as a whole. This is one worth planning a trip around. Just know it is busy, so room rates will reflect this. Also, be sure to make reservations for any restaurants on your "must eat at" list (frenchquarterfest.org).

New Orleans Jazz & Heritage Festival: Traditionally held the last weekend in April and the first weekend in May, this is the premier music festival in New Orleans, complete with local and internationally known artists as well as some of the best food in the city (nojazzfest.com). See the separate chapter on Jazz Fest.

MAY

Greek Festival: Greek food, live music, and family fun (gfno.com).

Bayou Boogaloo: Held along Bayou St. John, this music festival has become very popular among locals in recent years. Many craft homemade rafts and enjoy the music while floating on the bayou (thebayou boogaloo.com).

Mother's Day Celebration: Irma Thomas headlines the annual Mother's Day concert at the Audubon Zoo.

JUNE

Pride Festival: Events held throughout the French Quarter, including a parade. In 2021, the parade was replaced by a "krewe of house floats" where locals decorated their homes in honor of gay pride (neworleans pride.org).

Creole Tomato Festival: Held in the French Market, this festival includes the typical assortment of local music, food booths, and cooking demonstrations with a focus on the Louisiana Creole tomato (www.frenchmarket.org/creoletomatofest).

Louisiana Cajun and Zydeco Festival: Celebrates the traditions, food, and music of southwest Louisiana. This small festival is held just behind the French Quarter and is a fun one to check out if you happen to be in town (events.jazzandheritage.org).

JULY

Essence Festival: Typically held on the weekend nearest July 4, this very big festival highlights African-American musicians and culture. One feature that makes the event extra special is the free series of self-improvement seminars held at the Morial Convention Center.

Most concerts are at either the Smoothie King Center or the Superdome (essence.com/festival).

Bastille Day Fête: A celebration of New Orleans's French heritage, with cooking demonstrations, music, kids' activities, and more.

Running of the Bulls: A New Orleans take on the Spanish original. In this one, costumed runners are pursued by women on roller skates who hit the participants with plastic or inflatable bats (nolabulls.com).

Tales of the Cocktail: One of the premier events in the cocktail world, it draws mixologists and spirits aficionados from all over. Talks, tastings, and special events are held throughout the city (talesofthecocktail.org).

Grand Isle Tarpon Rodeo: America's oldest fishing rodeo, started in 1932 (tarponrodeo.org).

AUGUST

Satchmo Summer Fest: Celebration of New Orleans's native son (satchmosummerfest.org).

White Linen Night: An opportunity to wander the art galleries that line Julia Street, with live music in the street, champagne, and food from local restaurants. Attendees wear white linen in honor of the summer heat. After-party at the Contemporary Arts Center.

Red Dress Run: Annual event where thousands of men and women wear red dresses and "run" through the city, often while imbibing. Red dress runs were originally fairly small affairs hosted by local chapters of the Hash House Harriers, whose tagline is "a drinking club with a running problem." The New Orleans event has blossomed into one of the largest red dress runs anywhere.

SEPTEMBER

Southern Decadence: Held on Labor Day weekend, it's one of the largest LGBTQ+ events in the country (southerndecadence.net).

OCTOBER

Top Taco Fest: Taco festival including unlimited tacos and various tequilas as part of admission ticket (toptaconola.com).

JAZZ FEST

In this chapter we'll talk in detail about the **New Orleans Jazz & Heritage Festival,** known locally as Jazz Fest. We'll explore the music, the food, and the layout of the festival. I'll give you the insider tips that come from nearly 35 years of attending. You'll know what to bring, what to expect, how to create your own Jazz Fest plan, and everything else you need. I'll also help you enjoy a bit of Jazz Fest from wherever you are.

WHAT IS JAZZ FEST?

Officially, it's called the New Orleans Jazz & Heritage Festival. It's a seven-day festival of music, food, and crafts held at the New Orleans Fairgrounds in the Gentilly neighborhood of the city. Jazz Fest takes place the last weekend of April and the first weekend of May.

Jazz Fest is when people of all backgrounds and interests come together on the infield of the third-oldest horse track in the United States and simply enjoy life—enjoy each other, enjoy the music, and enjoy the food. The goodness that is New Orleans on a sun-drenched, music- and food-filled day. It's like Mardi Gras in that people you might not ever interact with on a daily basis are right there with you dancing, enjoying the vibe, looking out for each other on a long, hot day. It's those kinds of interactions that make New Orleans unique.

HISTORY OF JAZZ FEST

Jazz Fest was first held in April 1970, in Congo Square in the Tremé neighborhood, across Rampart Street, just "behind" the French Quarter. Back then what we now know as Congo Square was called Beauregard Square. Today it is an open space within Louis Armstrong Park.

George Wein, the force behind the Newport Jazz Festival, had been hired to create a festival unique to New Orleans. The idea was to celebrate New Orleans's heritage as the birthplace of jazz. Wein's vision was to hold a daytime heritage festival that would celebrate jazz as well as the culture of New Orleans. From the beginning his idea was to incorporate food, arts, and crafts along with the music. He also envisioned a series of nighttime concerts in addition to the daytime festival. One other thing he did was to hire two young people to help produce the show: Quint Davis and Allison Miner.

Jazz Fest Festival Stage JAMES CULLEN

Davis took a leading role and remains the producer of Jazz Fest today. He's the driving force behind the selection of artists and the creation of the schedules, not an easy feat with five days and a dozen stages, plus parades and arts and crafts demonstrations. Miner passed away in 1995, but among other things it was her idea to create the Music Heritage Stage, which is now the Allison Miner Stage in her honor.

That first festival was a five-day affair, held from April 22 to 26, 1970. It featured Mahalia Jackson and Duke Ellington, but also included Pete Fountain, Al Hirt, Fats Domino, Clifton Chenier, the Preservation Hall Band, The Meters, and many others. In a tradition that continues today, the Mardi Gras Indians were also featured.

That first festival had about 350 attendees. By comparison, there were nearly 700 musicians and other participants. In 1972 the organizers moved the festival to the fairgrounds, where it has been held to this day. By 1975 they had 80,000 attendees over the five days, and in 1976 the festival expanded to two weekends.

I started going to Jazz Fest in the mid-1980s as a high school kid. By 1989 more than 250,000 people attended over the course of the two weekends. It was either that year or the next I remember seeing the great Stevie Ray Vaughan. I remember thinking it was crowded, but I had no idea what was to come.

I went off to college in the late '80s and early '90s, but came home most every year for Jazz Fest. In 2001 I was in the largest crowd I had ever seen, to watch Dave Matthews perform. It was surreal in every way. Some 160,000 people jammed the fairgrounds that day: I think the previous record had been around 98,000. Dave Matthews was on one stage, while the rap artist Mystikal was on another. It was not a good idea logistically: we literally could not move.

Dave Matthews came on stage and it was an amazing scene. The roar of people singing along was like nothing I'd ever experienced. At one point Paul Simon and Lenny Kravitz joined Dave on stage. I still remember the look on Dave's face as he played "Me and Julio Down by the Schoolyard" with Simon. It was a look of absolute joy. It made the heat and the crowds absolutely worth it.

I share this story because it is so typical of Jazz Fest. To be sure, Jazz Fest is about the music, the food, the crafts, and the Mardi Gras Indians. But really, it is about the experience. Pretty much every year I have a moment or two where something magical happens. It could be small, like watching an old man grab a young coed's hand and teach her the two-step at the Fais Do-Do Stage, or it could be U2's guitarist the Edge jumping on stage in 2006 during the Dave Matthews Band's second visit to Jazz Fest and hearing 150,000 people all gasp at the exact same moment.

The 2006 Jazz Fest was special because it almost didn't happen. Katrina hit in August 2005 and the levee failures destroyed many parts of the city, including the Gentilly neighborhood where the fairground is. I remember there was lots of discussion about whether to hold Mardi Gras and Jazz Fest the following year. In the end both were held and were galvanizing events for New Orleanians.

On April 30, Bruce Springsteen played the big stage, known back then as the Acura Stage. He performed with the Seeger Sessions Band, and it was their first public gig together. So many moving moments in that set, but I still remember two very specifically.

One was when the Boss sang "My City of Ruins." It was written, of course, for his adopted hometown of Asbury Park, New Jersey, but he dedicated it to New Orleans. For as loud as the crowd had been at that very same stage a day earlier with Dave Matthews, it was completely silent as Bruce sang,

> There's a blood red circle on the cold dark ground
> And the rain is falling down
> The church door's blown open, I can hear the
> organ's sound
> But the congregation's gone . . .
> The boarded-up windows, the hustlers, and the
> thieves
> While my brother's down on his knees . . .
> Now tell now do I begin again?
> My city of ruins . . .
> Come on, rise up. Rise up!

I forget what came next, but it was upbeat. Everyone needed it. Near the end of his set, Bruce explained he had researched and found a couple lesser-known verses of "When the Saints Go Marching In." What he played was not the upbeat, bright "Oh when the Saints" we're used to hearing and singing. Instead he played it, complete with the additional verses, in what local music writer Keith Spera described as "an acoustic prayer." Spera, who has been covering music for decades, described that show as perhaps the best musical experience of his life.

I have one more special memory of that year. It was the New Orleans band Cowboy Mouth performing on the Gentilly Stage. That stage is on the opposite end of the fairgrounds from the big stage and is almost embedded into the neighborhood. I remember looking up as the band was playing and seeing the blue tarps over the roofs of the nearby houses: those tarps were everywhere in the city. Once again I was crying, but I was also incredibly happy to be there, celebrating life and music and rebirth and New Orleans.

OK, lots of history and memories, but we need to help you make the most of your Jazz Fest experience. Let's get into it.

WHICH WEEKEND TO ATTEND?

If you are coming into town for Jazz Fest, you also need to decide which weekend. Or take the week off in between and come for all of it!

If you do that, in between you could go to the crawfish festival over at NOLA Brewing usually held in the week between Jazz Fest. You could check out live music at the Maple Leaf Bar on Tuesday night, maybe get an early dinner at Jacques-Imo's right down the street. You could also take a day trip to Cajun country and visit Avery Island, home of Tabasco sauce, or just wander around, relax, and recharge.

The best choice is often just the weekend that best fits your schedule. Some people will choose based on the music. You can't go wrong—the music and food will be incredible on both weekends. My advice on this is know yourself: Do you like big crowds? Big-name acts? A specific style of music? Let these guide you.

Friday of week one and Thursday and Friday of week two will be less crowded than the Saturdays and Sundays. Saturdays are usually the biggest days. Even on the days with huge acts, you can find space at the other stages. If you are indifferent about one of the larger acts, that can be a great time to go check out artists you've never heard of. Don't overthink it.

WHERE TO STAY?

There are not many options close to the fairgrounds, with the exception of a couple of bed-and-breakfasts and the occasional Airbnb listing. However, the French Quarter is only 2.5 miles away, so an easy cab ride or rideshare. If you stay at one of the hotels on or close to Canal Street, hop on the streetcar, the red one. Take it to the end of the line (just follow everyone else that looks like they're going to the fest). You'll be right in front of City Park at Esplanade Avenue. Hop off and follow the crowd down Esplanade.

I recommend staying in the French Quarter, the Central Business District, or the Warehouse District. Basically, within walking distance of the Canal Street streetcar line and/or an easy cab ride to the festival. See the section on lodging at the beginning of this guide.

To recap the lodging, think about how you plan to get to the festival each day: Will you drive or take a rideshare, or do you want the streetcar to be an option? If you stay near Esplanade Avenue in the nearby Marigny or the downtown side of the French Quarter, you can walk down Esplanade to the festival. It's a bit dicey in a couple places, but you certainly wouldn't be the only one doing the walk.

TICKETS

You have several options, but let's cut to the chase. You want either single-day tickets or a Brass Pass. Basic one-day tickets are typically about $105 at the gate but tend to go up every year or two. You can get a discount if you buy ahead of time. If you live in town or know someone who does, there is typically a day (usually a Saturday) where you can purchase tickets at Tipitina's. You'll save some money on fees.

Whether in person or online, you want to get your tickets ahead of time. It's a major drag to be excited to get in and get your Jazz Fest started only to have to wait in line to buy tickets. This is especially true on days

Jazz Fest entrance **MARK BOLOGNA**

with a major headliner performing. You'll be shocked how early the big stage fills up.

Tickets for kids are $5 at the time of this writing, but you have to purchase them at the main gate.

If you plan on going every day, or even most days, you want the WWOZ Brass Pass. Brass Passes are transferable, include reentry, and cover all seven days of the festival. You also get access to the WWOZ tent, where you can get light refreshments, some shade, and access to private portalets. Your pass also gets you a year's membership to WWOZ, which helps support their ability to continue to operate.

WWOZ is a local radio station, located at 90.7 on the FM dial. More specifically, it is the Jazz & Heritage station, a community radio station based in the French Quarter and governed by the Jazz & Heritage Foundation. When they first started, back in 1980, they broadcast from a storage room upstairs at Tipitina's. DJs would occasionally drop a mic through a hole in the floor and broadcast performances live. Their aim is to be the worldwide voice of New Orleans.

If you can't make it to New Orleans for the festival, why not throw a Jazz Fest party? Turn on WWOZ online, cook up some red beans or jambalaya, invite some friends over, and there you go.

Pre-Katrina, Jazz Fest was cheap. At its peak, it was about $25 a day and you could always find discounted tickets. While those days are long gone, I do think you still get your money's worth today. The sheer quantity and breadth of music on any given today is terrific. I also understand, though, at $105 or more a person per day, Jazz Fest is now out of range for some people, particularly locals. That stinks.

If you are local, want to go, and can't afford the price, consider volunteering. Yes, you have to work, but you are on the grounds and get to enjoy the music and the people-watching. Usually, you work a four-hour shift and then have the rest of the time to yourself.

There are a couple VIP ticket options available, but I don't think they're worth it. If you are interested, head over to nojazzfest.com.

To recap: Buy your tickets ahead of time. The daily passes are sold by the weekend, so if you go online, you'll buy individual tickets for either the first or second weekend. If you want to buy a Brass Pass, go to WWOZ.org. If you want one of the VIP ticket packages, go to the Jazz Fest website at nojazzfest.com.

GETTING TO AND FROM

You've figured out when you are coming and you've got a place to stay. If you are taking the streetcar or a rideshare, you know what to do. But what if you are going to drive? There is limited parking on-site, but you don't want to do that. Basically, you need to purchase those parking packages with one of the VIP tickets I mentioned earlier. And if you stay until the end of the last act, you'll be trying to drive out along with everyone else.

If you are going to drive to Jazz Fest, here are some tips. Get there early—no later than 12 noon on weekdays and earlier on the weekends. The music starts at 11 a.m. and they sometimes open the gates earlier. If there is a big act scheduled, people will start to queue up early.

Parking is easier to come by on the back side of the track. Let me orient you. The long stretches of the track basically run east to west. The south side is roughly parallel to Esplanade Avenue and is where the main entrance is. On the north side, the back side, is the paddock entrance. De Saix Boulevard is parallel to this side. This is the area where you'll have the best success finding parking *if* you get there early.

A few blocks farther away is City Park. Again, you'll find parking in and just outside the park if you get there early in the day. Another option is to park on Wisner Avenue down towards Lake Pontchartrain and take the paid shuttle. Get there early if you are going to drive and find parking. If you can't get there early, don't drive. You might get lucky, but more than likely you'll just get aggravated.

If you do drive, keep a few things in your car for afterwards. An ice chest with cold water, Gatorade, or sodas. A snack like peanut butter and crackers, some fruit, or even some chips or peanuts are a good idea. A couple of towels and a change of clothes. It rains some years at Jazz Fest—this is late spring in New Orleans, after all, so you might be wet. You'll almost certainly be sweaty and a bit dirty, since Jazz Fest takes place on a horse track

If you're a diehard like me, you very likely might be heading out to dinner then to hear more music. You may not want to take the time to go back to your hotel. A little bit of planning ahead of time can help you make a smooth transition from Jazz Fest to after-fest each day.

One last thought: New Orleans has become a bicycling town. There are places at Jazz Fest where you can lock up your bike. There are no valets, but the area is manned by volunteers.

JAZZ FEST TOOLKIT

Get a festival map. Jazz Fest has 12 primary stages, several areas of food vendors, an arts fair, a folklife village, and numerous other things to see and experience. While the best way to experience the festival is to wander around, the map will come in handy. You can find one in the Jazz Fest program, but get one for free online or in the free local paper, the *Gambit*.

You need a list of artists by stage and time. The "cubes" are the only way to go. A Jazz Fest creation, the cubes are a sheet for each day presented in a grid and displaying the times, the stage names, and the artists. They make it easy to see who's playing where, and at what time. Again, you can find them in the *Gambit* pullout and on the Jazz Fest website. I print one for each day, but my favorites come from the *Gambit*. You can find them all over town, in grocery stores and drugstores, plus in plenty of casual restaurants. The *Gambit* editions have a cartoon-like quality to them. I usually bring the entire edition of *Gambit* in my backpack so I can read about the artists and have the cubes. It's just one of my traditions. New Orleans and Jazz Fest are all about traditions.

Download the free Jazz Fest app. I use the paper cubes throughout the day, but the app is good to have. If nothing else, it's a good way to keep track of the artists you would like to see.

Wear comfortable shoes or sandals. You're going to do a lot of walking. I wear flip-flops mostly because I like to kick them off once we get settled in to listen to an artist. Also, if it's a little wet or a little dusty, I just find it more comfortable. It's a horse track. You'll be walking in dirt, grass, sand, and, if it rains a lot, hay and water.

One caveat on the shoes: If it rains a lot and the grounds are likely to be flooded, you want rain boots, shrimp boots, or black rubber boots. Several years ago it stormed in the days leading up to Jazz Fest. I waited until the last minute to get boots for my wife and me, and ended up spending an afternoon traveling around the city to find them. The fairgrounds can be an absolute mess if we get a couple of days of hard rain. When you combine those conditions with a horse track *and* a couple hundred thousand people over several days, it gets sloppy. Sometimes they put hay and sand down, but truthfully it's better when they leave it as a swamp and you just dress for it.

Wear shorts or a skirt, but not jeans or long pants. It's hot. Be comfortable.

Don't forget a hat and sunglasses. The average high temperature in New Orleans in April is 77 degrees and in May 85 degrees, but it can certainly be hotter. You can usually count on sunny days at Jazz Fest. There's not much shade when you are out on the infield of the track, so you need protection from the sun. We'll cover some ways to get out of the heat, but be prepared.

Bring water. There's a long list of things you can't bring into the festival grounds, including alcohol. However, many years ago after a particularly hot Jazz Fest, the organizers relaxed the rules and allowed patrons to bring in sealed bottles of water. What we do is take several of the

Jazz Fest high steppin' MARK BOLOGNA

20-ounce bottles, say two per person, and freeze them overnight. We wrap them in a bandana or small towel and toss them in our backpack. That way, we have something to cool off with and we have cold water for most of the day.

There are fountains where you can refill your bottles, and you can purchase water as well. If you forget, you'll undoubtedly see people selling cold bottles of water as you walk to the entrance gates each day. They'll also be selling beer as you leave!

Don't forget your ID and a credit card. Jazz Fest went cashless as of 2023.

Cell phone, **battery pack**, **and cables.** It's the world we live in today: you'll be using your phone to check the app, to text the other members of your party who went to another stage, or to ask your spouse to grab one more meat pie and an extra beer on their way back to meet you. Your phone is going to die without extra power. You've been warned. One other thing here: on the busiest days, your texts and calls likely won't go through. They set up extra towers on-site, but you are in an environment with as many as 150,000 people, nearly all of whom are sending texts or using social media to send pictures all day long.

A couple of ziplock bags. We use the quart-size freezer bags. You'll want something to cover your phone, money, paper cubes, etc., in the event of rain. Even if not, it gets dusty, so it's not a bad idea to have the bags. Just stash a couple in your tote bag or backpack.

A small backpack. We end up with a decent amount of stuff with us. The backpack is a must when we go. Some people can travel lighter, but that's not our style. Most days we are out there with a group, so after we set up folding chairs, we just leave the bag there for the day. Even when you don't know anyone, you will find your neighbors are very friendly. Jazz Fest has a great community vibe, and everyone tends to look out for each other.

The following items are optional:

Towel, sheet, or bag chair. If it is just you or you and other adults, I might skip this and just plan on standing or sitting on the grass, unless you are the type who will park yourself at one stage for several hours. If you have small kids with you, or you do plan on parking at one of the stages, it is nice to have something to sit on. For the kids, it is good to have a picnic cloth of some sort. I've also seen people with kids bring some sort of small shelter to keep them out of the sun.

Camera. Most everyone has a camera on their phone, which is more than enough for taking pictures of you and your group. However, if photography is your jam, Jazz Fest is a visual feast.

Rain poncho or large garbage bag. It is not uncommon to have rainy days at Jazz Fest. A poncho, raincoat, or garbage bag will keep you dry and provide something to sit on if the rain stops.

A note on what not to bring: There's a long list on the Jazz Fest website, most of which is not surprising. No alcohol, drugs, or weapons. No outside food, though you can get away with a little bit and certainly snacks for the kids.

THE STAGES

By this point, you've figured out where to stay, how to get to the festival, and what to bring when you head out each day. Let's jump into the actual festival!

There's a lot going on once you get in the gates. Let's start with the music, and here's where the cubes we mentioned earlier, plus a festival map, come in handy. There are 12 stages, including some that are under large tents. The following seven stages are on the infield of the track.

Festival Stage: This is where most of the big acts perform. You'll see people camped out most of the day waiting for them. This area is also a visual treat: hundreds of flags flying above the crowds, as a beacon for friends to find each other.

Jazz Fest Heritage Stage MARK BOLOGNA

Gentilly Stage: Big acts later in the day, with a New Orleans bent most of the time. The better-known local acts will play here.

Congo Square: This stage leans towards African-American and international artists. It is part of the "big three" and will host some of the largest acts each season.

Fais Do-Do Stage: Primarily zydeco and Cajun music. If nothing else on the schedule appeals to you, head to the Fais Do-Do. It is my favorite of all the stages. There are always people dancing, you are close to the stage and the artists, and there is plenty of room to sit.

Jazz & Heritage Stage: A gem of a stage with a variety of music and performances by the Mardi Gras Indian tribes.

Economy Hall Tent: Traditional jazz music.

Kids Tent: This is a small area tucked inside the track near the grandstands. It includes musical acts and lots of activities for the kids. It is not crowded and tends to be a good spot to get away from the noise and crowds, with or without children.

Beyond the track but still within the confines of the fairgrounds are three big, white tents. These are the Jazz Tent, Blues Tent, and Gospel Tent. They each hold a couple thousand people, though they do get packed. Volunteers will help you find individual seats when it is crowded, and sometimes you can find a spot just outside to set up your bag chair.

The big tents all have misters. All tents except the Kids Tent also have folding chairs laid out in rows. Some tents have bleachers. Many of the most electric performances of the festival take place in these tents. The who's who of New Orleans musicians tend to play here. Even if you don't know the music, go on in. I try to hit at least one tent a day, and try to mix it up over the course of the festival.

In the grandstand are the Lagniappe and the Allison Miner stages. The **Lagniappe Stage** is actually outdoors in a kind of breezeway area. There's a lot of shade here, and as the name implies, a little bit extra. This stage tends to have a wide mix of music but is always a lot of fun and a great place to hear something new.

The **Allison Miner Music Heritage Stage** is one of my favorites for several reasons. For one, it's indoors, so it is a nice place to get a break from the sun and the heat. Or the rain! It is in the stands, so there are typical seats: plastic seating with the seats that pop up when you get out of them. It's air-conditioned. The best bathrooms are the ones up behind the seating area. You can count on them to be the least crowded, plus they are actual bathrooms as opposed to portalets. Another thing about this stage that you wouldn't know unless you wandered up there is the view. The front is all glass, so you get a great view of the festival from above.

However, none of this is why I love the stage. I love it because of the intimacy. The stage itself is very small, maybe 15 by 20 feet, maybe smaller. There will be an interviewer and the artist, who will usually perform a song or two as part of the discussion. Several years ago I saw Dr. John on this stage. He played just a bit, one song I think, but told many stories and answered questions from the crowd. Locals know this stage, but many others do not. Definitely check it out.

The grounds of the festival are expansive, and yet some of the stages can feel quite intimate. The Fais Do-Do Stage, located between the Congo Square and Gentilly stages, is one. It draws relatively large crowds but the placement makes it feel small.

Again, what you really want to do is get your hands on the cubes. This is my number-one tip for enjoying Jazz Fest. These are the printed schedules showing the acts by time and by stage for each day. The cubes are your Rosetta stone for Jazz Fest. The app is useful, but I want to see the paper cubes: I mark them up before leaving home each day, then keep them in my pocket. They are also useful for helping others who will invariably ask who's playing where, and when. You'll look like an insider when you casually pull out the cubes and point at them like a map.

A couple overall tips about the music and the stages: Get out of your comfort zone. Try to see at least one artist on each stage. It's probably not possible if you only go for a day, but definitely doable if you are at Jazz Fest for two or three days. They each have their own feel, and many are focused on a specific genre like traditional jazz or gospel. At a minimum spend some time at Fais Do-Do, duck in the Gospel Tent, go to the Jazz & Heritage Stage. Every year I stumble upon something that is unexpected and delightful, even after nearly 35 years of festivals.

I love to see the big acts, but every year I try to find at least one performer per day that I don't know. Those are often the best moments. Several years ago, I was at the Fais Do-Do—my go-to stage if nothing else lights me up. I looked at the cubes and saw a band called Johnnyswim was playing at the Gentilly Stage close by. I wandered over, ended up very close to the stage, and witnessed what was probably my favorite set of the year. Johnnyswim is a duo, a married couple. She is Amanda Sudano, the daughter of Donna Summer, and he is Abner Ramirez. Together their sound is the most intimate, interwoven, lovely expression I've heard in a while. I had no idea who they were or what their music was like, but I wandered over and was mesmerized. Now I'm a fan.

FOOD

More than 50 food options are scattered throughout the fairgrounds, but there are two large banks of food tents. One is behind the lagoon that is stage right of the Festival Stage. The second large area is in front of both the Jazz & Heritage Stage and the Economy Hall Tent.

Everyone has their favorites, but here's my list:

Natchitoches meat pies: Small, fried pies containing ground pork and beef, crawfish, or broccoli and cheese. Try them all, and consider bringing something to put a few in. Even a plastic grocery bag—you won't be the only one. The pies hold up well throughout the day and are a good treat to bring back to your friends who are holding your place at one of the big stages. My family laughs at me, but for years I've lined the pockets of my cargo shorts with foil: this way the meat pies stay warm, and I don't get the grease on my clothes. Definitely my favorite Jazz Fest food.

Crawfish Monica at Jazz Fest MARK BOLOGNA

Crawfish Monica: Crawfish tails in a rich, cheesy, spicy sauce mixed in with spiral pasta. A Jazz Fest tradition.

***Cochon de lait* po-boy:** Another favorite, roasted pig on a po-boy. This is a good one if you or the little ones are not too adventurous.

Vaucresson's hot sausage: Vaucresson's is the only original vendor from the first year of the festival, and that's no accident. Vance Vaucresson continues his father's tradition of serving up sausage po-boys at the fest. For more about Vance and his family business, check out episode 20 of the *Beyond Bourbon Street* podcast.

Roman Candy: Normally sold from a wooden cart pulled along the streets of New Orleans by a mule, this is a cheap and sweet taffy-like treat. At Jazz Fest you'll find the cart not far from the back of the crowds gathered at the Gentilly Stage and close to another favorite and cheap treat:

Plum Street Sno-Balls. There are three sno-ball stands on the grounds, but Plum Street is my favorite.

Jazz Fest strawberry lemonade **MARK BOLOGNA**

Strawberry lemonade: Rumor has it, this tastes good with your favorite whiskey if you manage to bring in a small, airplane-type bottle.

Herbal tea: Not my cup of tea, but a favorite of my wife's and nearly everyone else I know.

Crawfish bread: Bread stuffed with crawfish and cheese. Need I say more?

Combo plate with crawfish sack, oyster patties, and shrimp beignets, from Patton's caterers.

Ya-ka-mein: Not the best in the heat, but if you've never had this, do it. Ya-ka-mein is a beef broth–based soup with noodles, a boiled egg, maybe a little chicken, some beef, lots of spices, and green onions. It is vaguely Asian, but locals know it as a New Orleans thing. It's the kind of soup you'd get at a corner store in a Styrofoam cup. It is known as a hangover aid, and is popular outside of bars.

Miss Linda normally sells this out of the back of a truck, but for Jazz Fest she has a booth. Seriously, people will usually call it Miss Linda's ya-ka-mein. This is also a good dish to keep in mind if you get caught out at Jazz Fest during one of those rainy days when it can also get a little chilly.

Beignets: A nice, cheap change of pace. These are located behind the art vendors and never seem to have a long line. My friend Jenn usually eats as many beignets over the course of the festival as I eat meat pies.

Mango freeze: The other entry from my wife. You can find this booth over near the Fais Do-Do and the Gentilly stages. There is also a big oak tree nearby, one of the few places with natural shade on the infield of the track.

These are just my favorites and the can't-miss dishes. There are dozens more. Explore, eat, sample. Make a friend and share.

OTHER TIPS AND SUGGESTIONS

Beer: Beer stands are scattered throughout the festival grounds. However, if you want a draft beer, head over to the area just outside the Blues Tent. If you bring a backpack, stash an insulated bag in there, especially if you are going with a group and plan on drinking a lot. Buy canned beer and ask for some ice.

Bathrooms: Porta-potties are scattered around the actual racetrack. The best (cleanest and shortest lines) ones are the bunch located behind the crowds at the Gentilly Stage close to the grandstand. On the track near the Congo Square Stage there are portable, trailer-type restrooms for women. The best bathrooms are inside the grandstand, and upstairs behind the seating area at the Allison Miner Stage. When you do go to the porta-potties on the track, aim for the middle ones. There are nearly always shorter lines at those.

Food: Eat, a lot. If you see someone eating something that looks good, ask them about it. If they are a local, you'll probably get a couple good stories and they might even ask if you want a bite. Know yourself. If creamy foods or fried foods tend to upset your stomach, be cautious. It is usually hot at Jazz Fest, and food, drinks, and heat don't agree with everyone.

Shade: It gets hot and sunny at Jazz Fest. Insiders know there are several ways to escape the sun and sometimes the heat.

On the infield there is a large tree near the back of the viewing area at the Gentilly Stage. Get there early or go on a weekday. Another tree is near the Folklife Village with views of the Fais Do-Do Stage. This gets fairly crowded, but it's a good place to be. The mango freeze booth is also close by.

The tents will get you out of the sun. They have folding chairs, and most have misters.

The grandstand is air-conditioned, and there are exhibits to see on the main floor. Lines for the women's bathroom there are crazy. Go upstairs to the Allison Miner Stage for the best bathrooms, plus a hidden gem of a stage, as we discussed earlier. There are also some tables at the top of the grandstand behind the tiered seats if you just need a break.

The Lagniappe Stage, located in a breezeway area just after you walk under the grandstand, has seating, much of which is shaded. There are also nooks and crannies where you can set up your bag chair.

Jazz Fest clothing: In the middle of the infield is a tent selling Jazz Fest–themed clothing. Known as Bayou Wear or How Ah Ya shirts, each year there is a new theme. You'll see thousands of people wearing shirts from past years. My favorite is one with a red beans and rice pattern, complete with plastic red beans for buttons. There are also sundresses and skirts in the same pattern for women. This is the same tent where you'll find the Jazz Fest posters, which are the most collected poster series in the world.

Don't get wed to the big acts: The best finds are often the artists that are new to you. And, if you don't like an act, move along. There's so much to explore.

Visit the Louisiana Folklife area: Each weekend has a different set of artisans demonstrating their crafts. A nearby area is dedicated to Native Americans and specifically those tribes recognized as Louisiana tribes.

Check out the infield cutouts: Wander past the food booths and onto the infield, and you'll find large wooden cutouts. (In some years they are in different locations.) These honor the longtime greats of New Orleans and Jazz Fest who've left this world and moved on to higher ground. They include legendary musicians like Al Hirt and one of the original food vendors, Sonny Vaucresson. Sonny's son Vance continues the tradition of serving Vaucresson's sausage po-boys at the fest. The most recent addition to the cutouts is Jimmy Buffet, who was a big fan of Jazz Fest and a frequent performer.

A couple other tips: If you want to go out to dinner after a day at the festival, make reservations ahead of time—preferably before you even come in town. If you decide to go somewhere without reservations, leave the fest a little early: 5:30 or 6 p.m. This is especially true if you decide to go to a New Orleans institution like Jaques-Imo's in the River Bend area on Oak Street.

If you're new to Jazz Fest, make sure to enjoy the festivities as you enter on the Esplanade side of the fairgrounds. We usually come in through the paddock on the other side because we have off-street parking in that neighborhood, but it's more festive at the main gates. Plus, you can enjoy the street parties and grab a beer or a Bloody Mary at Liuzza's on your way in. Afterwards, you'll find impromptu front porch parties, often with bands.

The kids section is small, but very well done with lots of activities and music.

If you want the full-on immersive experience, plan on grabbing dinner after the fest then heading out to take in more music. There are plenty of shows and many places will have two shows a night, so you can easily stay out until 2 or 3 in the morning. I remember one year, maybe the first year we took our friend Jenn with us to Jazz Fest. We went all day, then headed over to Carrollton Station. I went to grab drinks and when I came back my girlfriend, now my wife, as well as Jenn were both nearly asleep. Jazz Fest is a marathon, my friends. Pace yourself accordingly.

DAY TRIPS & OVERNIGHT EXPLORATIONS

PLANTATIONS

Plantations lined the Mississippi River from below the French Quarter to well above Baton Rouge, Louisiana, in the late 1700s and early to mid 1800s.

For context, New Orleans was one of the largest cities in the country immediately after the Louisiana Purchase. It was important: river traffic was the main way of getting goods out of the middle of the United States to ports around the world. Plantations were almost like storefronts. Traders would come down the river, dock at a plantation, and buy, sell, and trade goods. Prior to the invention of the cotton gin and figuring out how to granulate sugar, the plantation crops were indigo, corn, and rice.

Plantations had slaves from the beginning and were a part of the original construct and planning for New Orleans. Forced labor was seen as one of many necessary supplies.

Today there are 13 plantations open to the public in some capacity. If you drive, you'll notice there are many more. Some are privately owned and serve as residences; others are abandoned and in decay.

You'll also note the ride is sometimes scenic and at other times disturbing. River Road has no clear view of the Mississippi. The levee is surprisingly low in some places, especially compared to the New Orleans side of the river. As you travel, you'll notice the poverty and decay, as well as the many oil refineries and fertilizer plants that give this area the unfortunate nickname "Cancer Alley."

I know that a visit to River Road is high on many people's lists when they visit Louisiana, so I want to help guide you. Yes, the plantations are splendid and full of history and grandeur. At the same time, the historical side of plantations is important. Too many visitors, in my opinion, go for the grandeur and miss the fact these plantations all thrived on the backs of the enslaved.

How do we resolve these two things? What about the people who grew up on the plantations, years after the end of slavery?

There are several ways to visit the plantations along River Road. Think about what you want to get out of your trip, and how much time you have. Do you want to learn about slavery? Gain an understanding of running a plantation? Admire the opulence? Learn about certain architectural styles? The history? The people who lived on these plantations?

WHAT TO EXPECT

Here's a quick list of things to consider in planning a visit:

- There are 13 plantations open to the public between New Orleans and Baton Rouge.
- Some are open during a set of hours, while others require an advance reservation.

- You definitely want to check hours of operation before you go.
- Some have general tours on certain days, and have special hours for school groups or bus tours.
- Expect to pay about $20 per person, per tour.
- Discounts are often available, and many bus tours include the price.
- Some plantations have self-guided tours of the grounds at reduced or no cost.
- The extent to which the tour addresses slavery varies considerably.
- The focus of each is different, and continues to evolve.
- There are options to stay overnight at some of the locations.
- Some offer food service and/or picnic grounds.
- The experience and emotions are going to vary quite a bit; be mindful of this with you, with kids, and with others.
- Allot 90 minutes to 2 hours per stop.
- Arrive at least 30 minutes prior to your tour.
- You could do two in a day, maybe three.

You have two options for getting there: a bus tour/private tour or a car. Rideshares do not consistently go out to the plantations, and if you do find one willing to take you out there, you probably won't find one to pick you up and return you to New Orleans.

DAY TRIPS

Group 1: Half-Day Trips

If you have only half a day, you'll want to go to one of these. They are the closest to New Orleans and are about a 30- to 45-minute drive from Downtown.

Destrehan Plantation is close to New Orleans and holds a document signed by Thomas Jefferson and James Madison. Tour guides are in costume. *Interview with a Vampire* and *12 Years a Slave* were filmed here. It is 10 miles from the airport, so you could visit during a long layover.

The house itself was originally built in the French Creole style, but renovated to Greek Revival in 1840. Due to its close proximity to New Orleans, it can get crowded during peak hours.

Ormond Plantation has a bed-and-breakfast. Originally built around 1789, it was sold in 1805 to Richard Butler, who renamed it after his ancestral home in Ireland. Tours by appointment. Tour guides are not in costume, it is not as crowded as some others, and you can have lunch at the plantation, which is not an option at all of them.

Group 2: Daylong Trips

These are 45 to 60 minutes from New Orleans and where I would focus a daylong trip. I would start with Whitney Plantation, then pick one or two of the following depending on your interests: Oak Alley, Laura, St. Joseph's, San Francisco, or Evergreen.

Note: If you drive and need a place for lunch, try B&C Seafood in Vacherie.

In my opinion, **Whitney Plantation** is the one you should visit above any others if you decide to visit any plantations at all. It is the only plantation solely focused on the lives of the enslaved. Most of the tour is outdoors, with little focus on the plantation house itself. There is a very moving exhibit on the Slave Revolt of 1811. The tour includes a visit to the slave cabins, a chapel, and a discussion of the processing of sugarcane.

We did a three-part series on plantations on the *Beyond Bourbon Street* podcast, with an entire episode devoted to Whitney (episode 54). The visit and the interview completely changed the way I view the plantations, as well as my understanding of what life was like for the enslaved. I encourage you to give it a listen.

Oak Alley Plantation is the most well-known, and is therefore a very popular stop. The house tour is excellent. The slavery exhibit is housed in the slave cabins and is very good, but is self-guided and not a part of the main house tour. Overnight accommodations are available, as is a casual restaurant that serves an excellent gumbo.

Oak Alley is a good example of the influence Whitney has had on the other plantations. Until recently, tour guides at Oak Alley wore period dress and barely mentioned slavery. The costumes are now gone and the tour has been revised to include at least some discussion of the enslaved.

Laura Plantation is a French Creole plantation that has been owned by four generations of the same family. This tour also includes the slave quarters and offers a balanced approach to the history of plantations.

St. Joseph's Plantation is a working sugarcane plantation owned by the same family since 1877. The focus of their tour is on Reconstruction.

San Francisco Plantation is the most colorfully painted plantation. It was completed in 1856 in a style called Steamboat Gothic.

Evergreen Plantation is one of the largest intact plantation complexes and was owned by Ambroise Heidel, who also owned Whitney.

The main building dates to 1790 and includes 22 slave cabins on the grounds.

Group 3: Specialty Plantations

This is what I would describe as a specialty group. Each has something unique about it. These plantations are one to two hours away from New Orleans.

Nottoway Resort is 53,000 square feet of innovations and opulence. Built in 1859, it is the largest remaining plantation home in the American South. It has tour guides in costume and very little mention of slavery.

Houmas House Plantation is actually two main houses joined together. Its focus is on the life of an antebellum sugar baron. It features extensive gardens and has a restaurant serving lunch and dinner.

Poche Plantation was built after the Civil War in the Victorian Renaissance style of architecture. A former owner maintained a diary of the Civil War as a Confederate, written in French. There is bed-and-breakfast and an RV park on-site. The plantation originally grew sugarcane as its primary crop but then grew tobacco, which was unusual during that time period.

Magnolia Mound is in Baton Rouge and may be worth a stop if you are passing through, but is not worthy of a dedicated trip from New Orleans. It is small, rustic, and focused on antiques, though it does include exhibits about slavery.

IN A CATEGORY BY ITSELF: THE MYRTLES PLANTATION

The 13 plantations described in this section are the most commonly visited, and all in some way or another form a cohesive group, with the possible exception of Poche. However, the **Myrtles Plantation** deserves a separate discussion.

Located in St. Francisville, it is the plantation farthest from New Orleans if you travel via River Road. The small town is a good jumping-off spot for visiting Tunica Falls or the Angola prison museum, and just wandering the shops.

The plantation itself offers several different types of accommodations, an upscale restaurant, and a guided tour of the main house. Where it most differs from the other plantations is that is has carved out a niche as "the most haunted home in America." The Myrtles has been featured on numerous television shows that investigate ghosts and paranormal occurrences, and the tour plays up these aspects.

My wife and I spent two nights at the Myrtles and enjoyed the experience, though it was a bit terrifying.

GUIDED TOURS

While I focused the discussion above on the experience of driving, there are several guided plantation tours that include transportation, including the following:

Cajun Encounters (cajunencounters.com/tours/plantations; 504-834-1770) offers tours of Oak Alley, Laura, and Houmas House. You'll be transported via minibus from downtown New Orleans to the plantation(s) and tours you select. Along the way, a guide will share details of the area.

Cajun Pride Swamp Tours (cajunprideswamptours.com; 504-467-0758) offers tours of Oak Alley and Laura plantations, or a combination swamp and plantation tour. Travel by minibus with an experienced guide.

Gray Line (graylineneworleans.com/plantation-tours; 504-569-1401) visits Whitney, Laura, and Oak Alley plantations. Travel is usually by full-sized bus, though they may sometimes use minibuses.

OVERNIGHT ACCOMMODATIONS

The following plantations offer overnight accommodations:

Ormond: B&B featuring five rooms in the main house.

Oak Alley: Offers nine cottages with different configurations. Restaurant on-site.

Nottoway: A variety of accommodations in multiple buildings on the property. There is a restaurant, but it is closed for maintenance at the time of this writing.

Houmas House: Multiple rooms available and a restaurant.

Poche: An RV park and B&B.

CLOSING THOUGHTS ON PLANTATIONS

For me, the idea of radical empathy is important when visiting the plantations. It is beyond trying to walk in someone else's shoes. Rather, it is trying to walk in their shoes with their perspective. This is probably impossible to fully achieve, but trying leads to a better understanding. To visit plantations and only see the grandeur is to miss the dirty, horrible underpinnings. The foundation.

As my wife and I discussed our visits, two things kept coming up: the grandeur of the plantation homes themselves, against the reality that they were built on the backs of enslaved people. Keep this in mind as you plan your own visit.

LAGNIAPPE

AVERY ISLAND

Avery Island is home to Tabasco Hot Sauce. Located south of Lafayette, Louisiana, it is about 140 miles from New Orleans. The **Tabasco Museum** (tabasco.com/visit-avery-island/tabasco-tour) includes an excellent tour that talks about the history of the famous hot sauce, and the on-site restaurant is very good.

In addition to learning about Tabasco, the gem of the island is the **Jungle Gardens** (junglegardens.org). At the Jungle Gardens, you have the option of a guided tour or a self-guided driving tour. Either is fine, but the gardens are fun to explore. You'll see a large collection of plants, wildlife, and even a small Buddhist shrine.

Avery Island could be visited as a long day trip. If you decide to make it an overnight experience, consider a bed-and-breakfast in nearby Broussard, or spend the night in Lafayette.

SWAMP TOURS

In our Beyond Bourbon Street Facebook group, we often get asked about swamp tours. There are basically two or three varieties. The one most people think of involves a traditional boat or maybe an airboat with a large fan on the back. Tours such as these generally are focused on alligators and a discussion of swamps and their importance.

Many of these offer an opportunity to feed and perhaps even hold a baby alligator. While they are popular, I would recommend against any tour that offers feeding and/or holding of alligators. The reality is these are wild animals best left undisturbed. Seeing an alligator in its natural habitat is quite a thrill, and there are tour operators who will provide this experience. My recommendation for a tour via motorized craft is **Dr. Wagner's Honey Island Swamp Tours** (honeyislandswamp.com; 504-242-5877).

My personal preference and recommendation is to explore the swamps via a kayak or canoe tour. You will be closer to the water, and the slower movement means an opportunity to see and learn about the swamp in a way you just don't get zipping around in a motorized craft. Two operators that do an excellent job are **Honey Island Kayak Tours** (honeyislandkayaktours.com) and **Canoe and Trail Adventures** (canoeandtrail.com).

Most tours focus on either the Honey Island Swamp or Manchac Swamp. They are in different directions from each other, but both are about 45 minutes from downtown New Orleans. Many tour companies offer transportation or will work with you to arrange transportation if you don't have a car. Rideshares and taxis are not an option.

Pirates Alley **JAMES CULLEN**

ACKNOWLEDGMENTS

Writing a book is hard. Thank you to my wife, Marie. You've been there every step of the way to encourage me, and to keep the children at bay so I could spend the time needed to get to the finish line. Your love and friendship mean the world to me. The last 27 years have been a wonderful, crazy, unpredictable journey. There is no one else I would want by my side. I love you more than you know.

To my twin daughters, Sophia and Olivia. You supported me throughout, first by asking why I was writing a book then by offering a steady stream of content ideas (sadly, neither Harper, our cat, nor Mona Lisa, our dog, merit their own sections despite your lobbying). Olivia, your hugs and encouragement were more important than you could know. Sophia, your setting of daily word goals made a real difference. You were quite the task master! Love you two to Pluto and back.

To my parents, Jan and Vincent Bologna. First, thanks for having me! Your never-ending love and constant words of encouragement have been so important. Mom, I appreciate the constant ideas and the gentle constructive criticism of the podcast that was so instrumental to the creation of this book.

My mother-in-law, Beata Willison. You've been such an enthusiastic supporter and found a way to help me along even when I doubted myself. Thank you.

My brother, Matthew, my sister, Natasha, and their spouses, Kate and Mike. The calls and notes of encouragement meant so much. Natasha, your ideas and checking in on the progress made a difference.

Scott Willison, my brother-in-law. Thanks for the support and the friendship.

To my extended family, including aunts, uncles, and cousins. The joy of a large family is having plenty of people to check in and offer words of support!

A special word to my deceased grandmother, Dorothy Vicknair. You've been gone for a long time, but I inherited your curiosity about this place we call home. I wish you and Paw Paw were here to see this book get published.

To my friend and literary agent, Sally Ekus. You cautioned me against writing a book, then whole-heartedly encouraged and pushed me when the time was right. You've served not only as my agent but, more importantly, as my friend and chief cheerleader.

To my editor, Greta Schmitz, for believing in this project!

To my friends Chris and Jennifer Marshall. You're such an important part of our lives. From naming the podcast (Jenn) to reading pieces of the draft (Chris), your love and support have made this possible.

Dave Leonard, you've been one of my closest friends for 25 years. You've offered not only support but a genuine interest in the project. Thanks for encouraging me even when I wanted to quit.

Camp and Kay Morrison, you're the best neighbors ever. You were both so supportive of this book. I appreciate the steady flow of suggestions, the checking in on the progress, and the willingness to entertain our kids when I needed space to write.

Elizabeth Pearce, your experience as an author, a business owner, and my friend and accountability partner played an important role in this book. Thanks for answering my repeated questions.

James Cullen and Susan Whelan, I met you both through the wacky world of social media, but you've become close friends. Your honesty and pushing of me throughout this project have been instrumental. James's photography work can be seen throughout this book

To my therapist, Dr. Allyson Bennett. Mental health is so important and yet still so stigmatized in our world. Our weekly sessions kept me on track and, most importantly, healthy. You told me when to push and when the book was good enough to hand over. I will forever be thankful to you.

The *Beyond Bourbon Street* podcast began as an idea in 2014 at an event called Podcast Movement. It was there I was introduced to my first mentor in the world of podcasting, Lou Mongello. Lou is host of the wildly popular Disney-focused podcast *WDW Radio*. From the moment he heard my idea, his eyes lit up, he offered to help in any way possible, and he has been a constant source of knowledge and support every day since. Along the way, I met Michael O'Neal, my longtime business coach. Mike is always reinventing himself, but his own podcast, *The Solopreneur Hour*, proved a valuable model.

The previously mentioned Lou Mongello hosts an annual event called Momentum. Through it I've made friends who have been supportive of all that I do, and especially of this book. Thanks to Fred Abeli, David Recchione, Jesse McCollough, Pete Bush, Tim Bigonia, Lisa DiNoto Glasser, Kristin Fuhrmann Simmons, Michelle Burdo Zimmerman, Jen Hoffman, Lauren Gaggioli, and everyone else who is a part of that community. Jen, our long talks and honest discussions about the ups and downs of business and life are pure energy for my soul.

And finally, thanks to the thousands of people who listen to *Beyond Bourbon Street* every other week. I've gotten to know many of you through Facebook and through your texts and emails, as well as your direct support via Patreon. I do this for you.

JAMES CULLEN

INDEX

D

E

L

M

N